Isaac H. Elliott

Record of the Services of Illinois Soldiers

In the Black Hawk War, 1831-32, and in the Mexican War, 1846-8

Isaac H. Elliott

Record of the Services of Illinois Soldiers
In the Black Hawk War, 1831-32, and in the Mexican War, 1846-8

ISBN/EAN: 9783337133801

Printed in Europe, USA, Canada, Australia, Japan

Cover: Foto ©ninafisch / pixelio.de

More available books at **www.hansebooks.com**

OF

ILLINOIS SOLDIERS

IN THE

BLACK HAWK WAR,

1831-32,

AND IN

THE MEXICAN WAR,

1846-8,

CONTAINING A COMPLETE ROSTER OF COMMISSIONED OFFICERS AND ENLISTED
MEN OF BOTH WARS, TAKEN FROM THE OFFICIAL ROLLS ON FILE
IN THE WAR DEPARTMENT, WASHINGTON, D. C.

WITH AN APPENDIX,

GIVING A RECORD OF THE SERVICES OF THE ILLINOIS MILITIA, RANGERS
AND RIFLEMEN, IN PROTECTING THE FRONTIER FROM THE
RAVAGES OF THE INDIANS FROM 1810 TO 1813.

PREPARED AND PUBLISHED BY AUTHORITY OF THE THIRTY-SECOND GENERAL ASSEMBLY,

By ISAAC H. ELLIOTT,

ADJUTANT-GENERAL OF THE STATE OF ILLINOIS.

SPRINGFIELD, ILL.:
H. W. ROKKER, STATE PRINTER AND BINDER.
1882.

CONTENTS.

	PAGE.
Introductory	IX

Historical Memoranda.

Black Hawk War	XI
Muster Roll Capt. Gholson Kercheval's company	XXIII
Mexican War	XXIV

BLACK HAWK WAR.

FIRST BRIGADE.

First Regiment.

Capt. John Bay's company	3
Capt. D. B. Russell's company	4
Capt. Achilles Coffee's detachment	5
Capt. Harrison Wilson's company	6
Capt. Joel Holliday's company	7
Capt. Achilles Coffee's company	8

Second Regiment.

Capt. George P. Bowyer's company	10
Capt. Wm. J. Stephenson's company	11
Capt. Obediah West's company	12
Capt. Charles Dunn's company	13
Capt. Jonathan Durman's company	14
Capt. Armstead Holman's company	14

Third Regiment.

Capt. Ardin Biggerstaff's company	16
Capt. John Onslott's company	17
Capt. James Hall's company	18
Capt. James N. Clark's company	19
Capt. Berryman G. Wells' company	20

Spy Battalion.

Capt. Wm. N. Dobbins' company	22
Capt. James Bowman's company	23

Detachments.

From Capt. W. S. Stephenson's company	25
From Capt. Charles Dunn's company	25
From Capt. Russell's company	26
From Capt. Arman's company	26
From Capt. West's company	26
From Capt. Holliday's company	26
From Capt. Bowyer's company	27

SECOND BRIGADE.

First Regiment.

Capt. Thomas B. Ross' company	28
Capt. Samuel Brimberry's company	29
Capt. Isaac Sanford's company	30
Capt. Robert Griffin's company	32
Capt. Jonathan Mayo's company	33
Capt. Royal A. Nott's company	34

CONTENTS.

Second Regiment.

	PAGE.
Capt. Alex. M. Houston's company	36
Capt. John Arnold's company	37
Detachment of Capt. Elias Jordan's company	38
Detachment of Capt. Highsmith's company	38
Detachment of Capt. Barnes' company	39

Third Regiment.

Capt. Solomon Hunter's company	40
Capt. Champion S. Mading's company	41
Capt. John Haynes' company	42
Capt. William Thomas' company	43
Capt. Daniel Powell's company	44
Detachment of Capt. Powell's company	45

Spy Battalion.

Capt. John F. Richardson's company	46
Capt. Abner Greer's Company	47
Capt. John McCann's company	48

Detachments.

Adjutant Parmenter's	50
Of Capt. Hiram Roundtree's company	50
Of Capt. Hiram Kinade's company	50
Of Capt. Mayo's company	50
Of Capt. Earl Pierce's company	51
Of Capt. Bennett Howlin's company	51
Of Capt. Sol. Hunter's company	51
Of Capt. J. F. Richardson's company	51
Of Capt. Isaac Sanford's company	51
Of Capt. Wm. Highsmith's company	51
Of Capt. A. M. Houston's company	52
Of Capt. John Barnes' company	52
Of Capt. Abner Greer's company	53

THIRD BRIGADE.

First Regiment.

Capt. David Smith's company	54
Capt. William Gillham's company	55
Capt. William Gorden's company	56
Capt. George F. Bristow's company	57
Capt. S. T. Matthews', afterwards J. T. Arnett's company	57
Capt. Walter Butler's company	58

Second Regiment.

Capt. Hiram Roundtree's company	60
Capt. James Kincaid's company	61
Capt. Gershom Paterson's company	62
Capt. Aaron Bannon's company,	63
Capt. Thomas Stout's company,	64

Third Regiment.

Capt. Andrew Bankson's company	66
Capt. Wm. Adair's company	67
Capt. Josiah S. Briggs' company	68
Capt. James Thompson's company,	69
Capt. Jacob Feman's company, afterward Capt. James Connor's company	70
Capt. James Burns' company	71

Fourth Regiment.

Capt. Bennett Nowlen's company,	73
Capt. Ozias Hail's company	74
Capt. Jesse Claywell's company	75
Capt. Reuben Brown's company	76
Capt. Thomas Moffett's company	77
Capt. Henry L. Webb's company	78

Spy Battalion:

Capt. Allen F. Lindsey's company	80
Capt. Samuel Huston's company	81

WHITESIDE'S BRIGADE.

First Regiment.

Capt. Julius L. Barnsback's company	83
Capt. John Thomas' company	84
Capt. John Tate's company	85
Capt. Josiah Little's company	86

CONTENTS. V

PAGE.

Second Regiment.
Capt. Thomas Chapman's company.. 88
Capt. Levi D. Boone's company.. 89
Capt. William G. Flood's company... 90
Capt. Benjamin James' company.. 91
Capt. Jeremiah Smith's company... 92

Third Regiment.
Capt. John Harris' company... 93
Capt. Benjamin Barney's company.. 94
Capt. Elisha Petty's company... 94
Capt. William B. Smith's company... 95
Capt. Nathan Winter's company.. 96

Fourth Regiment.
Capt. M. G. Wilson's company... 98
Capt. Wm. C. Hall's company.. 99
Capt. Abraham Lincoln's company.. 100

Fifth Regiment.
Capt. M. L. Covell's company... 102
Capt. Robert McClure's company... 105
Capt. J. C. Pugh's company... 103
Capt. John G. Adams' company... 104

Spy Battalion.
Capt. John Dawson's company.. 106
Capt. Thomas Carlin's company.. 107
Capt. John Dement's company.. 108

Odd Battalion.—Major James'.
Capt. Daniel Price's company... 110
Capt. Peter Warren's company... 111
Capt. Thomas Harrison's company.. 112

Odd Battalion.—Major Thos. Long's.
Capt. Jacob Ebey's company... 113
Capt. Japhet A. Ball's company... 114

Unattached Companies.
Capt. William Moore's company.. 116
Capt. John Winstanley's company.. 117
Capt. William T. Given's company... 118
Capt. Erastus Wheeler's company.. 118
Capt. Samuel Smith's, late Jacob Fry's company................................. 119
Capt. Thomas McDow's company... 120
Capt. David Crow's company... 121
Capt. L. W. Goodan's company... 122

FOURTH BRIGADE.

Fortieth Regiment (Militia.)—Commanded by Col. John Strawn.
Capt. Geo. B. Willis' company.. 124
Capt. Robert Barnes' company... 125
Capt. William M. Stewart's company... 126
Capt. William Haw's company.. 127

INDEPENDENT REGIMENTS.

Col. Isaac B. Moore's Regiment.
Capt. John B. Thomas' company.. 128
Capt. Alexander Bailey's company... 129
Capt. Eliakim Ashton's company... 130
Capt. Morgan L. Payne's company.. 131
Capt. James Palmer's company... 132
Capt. I. M. Gillespie's company.. 133
Capt. James Gregory's company.. 134
Capt. Corbin R. Hutt's company... 135

Twenty-seventh Regiment—Militia.
Capt. Milton M. Maugh's company.. 136
Capt. Nicholas Dowling's company... 138
Capt. Clack Stone's company.. 139
Capt. Charles McCoy's company.. 140
Capt. Benj. J. Aldenrath's company... 141

	PAGE.
Capt. H. H. Gear's company	142
Capt. Samuel H. Scale's company	144
Capt. Jonathan Craig's company	145
Capt. Lambert P. Vansburgh's company	146

ODD BATTALIONS.

Major N. Buckmaster's Battalion.

Capt. Holden Seisson's company	148
Capt. Joseph Napier's company	149
Capt. Aaron Armstrong's company	189

Odd Battalion of Rangers.

Capt. Abner Eads'	152
Capt. David W. Barnes' company	151
Capt. Asel F. Ball's company	153

Companies in Odd Battalions.

Capt. John Sain's company	155
Capt. William McMurtry's company	159
Capt. Asel F. Ball's company	150
Capt. J. W. Kenney's company	158
Capt. Peter Butler's company	156
Capt. James White's company	167

Odd Companies Attached to Col Dodge's Regiment.

Capt. James Craig's company	162
Capt. Enoch Duncan's company	163

COMPANIES UNDER GEN. ATKINSON.

Capt. William Gordon's company	166
Capt. Cyrus Matthews' company	167
Capt. George McFadden's company	168
Capt. Samuel Smith's company	168
Capt. B. James' company	169
Capt. John Stennett's company	170
Capt. M. L. Covell's company	171
Capt. John S. Wilbourne's company	172
Capt. Solomon Miller's company	173
Capt. Elijah Iles' company	174

INDEPENDENT COMPANIES.

Capt. Jacob M. Early's company	176
Capt. Seth Pratt's company	177
Capt. Alexander D. Cox's company	178
Capt. James Walker's company	179
Capt. William Warwick's company	179
Capt. Alex. M. Jenkins' company	180
Capt. B. B. Craig's company	181
Capt. William C. Ball's company	182
Capt. Alexander White's company	183
Capt. Charles S. Dorsey's company	184
Capt. A. W. Snyder's company	184
Capt. Earl Pierce's company	186

COMPANIES SERVING PREVIOUS TO 1832.

1827—Capt. James M. Strode's company	187

Major N. Buckmaster's Battalion, 1831.

Capt. Solomon Miller's company	188
Capt. William Moore's company	190

MEXICAN WAR.

FIRST CALL—ONE YEAR VOLUNTEERS.

First Regiment—Col. J. J. Hardin.

	PAGE.
Field and Staff	194
Capt. Morgan's Co. A	195
Capt. Smith's Co. B	196
Capt. Fry's Co. C	197
Capt. McConnel's Co. D	198
Capt. Robertson's Co. E	200
Capt. Crow's Co. F	201
Capt. Wyatt's Co. G	202
Capt. Montgomery's Co. H	204
Capt. Prentiss' Co. I	205
Capt. Mower's Co. K	206

Second Regiment—Col. Wm. H. Bissell.

Field and Staff	229
Capt. Coffee's Co. A	229
Capt. Carder's Co. B	231
Capt. Baker's Co. C	232
Capt. Wheeler's Co. D	234
Capt. Lott's Co. E	235
Capt. Hacker's Co. F	236
Capt. Lemen's Co. G	238
Capt. Raith's Co. H	239
Capt. Miller's Co. I	241
Capt. Starbuck's Co. K	242

Third Regiment—Col. Ferris Foreman.

Field and Staff	266
Capt. Stout's Co. A	267
Capt. Freeman's Co. B	268
Capt. McAdam's Co. C	270
Capt. Bishop's Co. D	272
Capt. Seller's Co. E	274
Capt. Campbell's Co. F	276
Capt. Lawler's Co. G	277
Capt. Hicks' Co. H	279
Capt. Harvey's Co. I	281
Capt. McGinnis' Co. K	283

Fourth Regiment—Col. E. D. Baker.

Field and Staff	285
Capt. H. A. Roberts' Co. A	285
Capt. Garret Elkin's Co. B	287
Capt. J. C. Pugh's Co. C	289
Capt. Achilles Morris' Co. D	291
Capt. Daniel Newcomb's Co. E	293
Capt. Asa D. Wright's Co. F	294
Capt. Edward Jones' Co. G	296
Capt. John S. McConkey's Co. H	298
Capt. John C. Hurt's Co. I	300
Capt. Lewis W. Ross' Co. K	301

SECOND CALL (DURING THE WAR.)

First Regiment (Fifth Illinois)—Col. E. W. B. Newby.

Field and Staff	208
Capt. Bond's Co. A	208
Capt. Cunningham's Co. B	210
Capt. Turner's Co. C	212
Capt. Moses' Co. D	214
Capt. Hook's Co. E	216
Capt. Kinney's Co. F	218

VIII   CONTENTS.

    Capt. Reed's Co. G... 220
    Capt. Hampton's Co. H... 222
    Capt. Niles' Co. I... 224
    Capt. Kinman's Co. K... 226

Second Regiment (Sixth Illinois)—Col. J. Collins.
    Field and Staff.. 244
    Capt. James Bowman's Co. A.. 245
    Capt. C. L. Wright's Co. B.. 247
    Capt. Harvey Lee's Co. C... 249
    Capt. John Bristow's Co. D... 251
    Capt. William Shepherd's Co. E.. 253
    Capt. David C. Berry's Co. F.. 255
    Capt. John M. Moore's Co. G.. 257
    Capt. James Burns' Co. H... 259
    Capt. Edward E. Harvey's Co. I.. 261
    Capt. John Ewing's Co. K... 263

INDEPENDENT COMPANIES.

Mounted Volunteers.
    Capt. A. Dunlap's company... 304
    Capt. W. B. Stapp's company.. 307
    Lieut. Lanphere's detachment.. 309
    Capt. M. K. Lawler's company.. 309
    Capt. Josiah Littell's company... 312

REGULAR ARMY ENLISTMENTS.

Fourteenth U. S. Infantry.
    "E" company... 314

Sixteenth U. S. Infantry.
    "A" company... 315
    "G" company.. 315, 316

INTRODUCTORY

Although many years have elapsed since the close of the Mexican War, and a much greater period of time since the Black Hawk War, the archives in the Adjutant-General's office have shown no record of the services of our soldiers in either of these wars. In fact, excepting the meagre and occasional rolls of the militia and riflemen, deposited by Governor Edwards' heirs some years ago, there has been, until quite a recent date, no record of the service of any Illinois soldiers in this office prior to the late War of the Rebellion. The organization of the society of the "Veterans of the Mexican, Black Hawk and Florida wars," in 1874, revived an interest in this subject, and the members have, at their annual reunions since that date, agitated the subject with more or less effect, until they have, no doubt, largely aided in securing their demands in the present publication. In 1877, Hon. Cornelius Rourke, a member of the House of Representatives, from Menard county, offered a bill to authorize the Governor to employ a clerk to transcribe these records from the official rolls of the War Department. This, however, did not become a law. This bill was, no doubt, offered in response to the action of the "Mexican War Veteran Association," which, at the September meeting previous, held at Springfield, had passed the following resolution:

Resolved, That it is the sense of the Mexican War Veterans, now in session at the State capital, that a commission should be appointed by the next Legislature of Illinois, with instructions to procure from the archives at Washington, D. C., all information, statistical and otherwise, relative to the operations of the troops from Illinois, and that said information be placed on file in the Adjutant-General's office in this State.

The Legislature, in 1879, added to the general appropriation bill a section authorizing the Governor to appoint a clerk to go to Washington and transcribe all the records, of both volunteer and regular soldiers from Illinois, in the Black Hawk or Mexican wars, and appropriated the sum of five hundred dollars for the purpose. (Laws 1879, p. 80.) In pursuance of this act, Governor Cullom appointed Col. Ferris Foreman, of Vandalia, late the Colonel of the Third Regiment Illinois volunteers and the only surviving Colonel of the Mexican War, to that duty. Col. Foreman proceeded to Washington, and in his report to the Governor, under date of December 16, 1879, states that he was denied the privilege of access to the records by the Adjutant-General, under the standing orders and regulations of the War Department, and reported that it would be necessary to have a resolution passed by Congress before access could be had to the rolls on file in the War Department. After the Hon. Robert T. Lincoln became Secretary of War, Governor Cullom, who has always taken an active interest in the effort to obtain these records for the State, visited him in Washington, and on the personal solicitation of the Governor, Secretary Lincoln was induced to cause these rolls to be transcribed by clerks in the War Department, and correct copies of all such have been furnished by him to this office, and are published complete in this book.

The section of the appropriation bill passed in 1881, which authorizes this publication, was drawn up and offered by the Hon. Samuel H. Martin, a member of the Thirty-second General Assembly from White county, himself a Lieutenant in the Fourteenth United States Infantry during the Mexican War, and to whose efforts, as well as to the efforts of the Honorable Secretary of War and His Excellency the Governor, the merit of obtaining and publishing these records is largely due.

Before commencing the preparation of this publication, an advertisement was inserted in all the leading newspapers of the State, requesting all persons in possession of facts or any data concerning the service of the Illinois soldiers in the Black Hawk and the Mexican wars, to communicate the same to this office. Quite a general response was made to this request by the surviving veterans of both wars, and much interesting and valuable material has been thus accumulated in this office, the larger portion of which cannot, of course, be used in the limits of a publication like the present. The thanks, however, of this office are due to those who so kindly responded to our request, and their communications have all been carefully preserved among the files of this office for future historical reference, and will make a fund of valuable military information for the use of the historian of the future.

Believing the intention of the General Assembly mainly met in the publication of the complete rosters, the briefest possible introductory sketch is made of the prominent facts of the Black Hawk war, which is compiled from Edwards' History of the State of Illinois, and other trustworthy sources, including the correspondence before mentioned. This is followed by a short historical sketch of the part taken by the various commands of Illinois volunteers in the Mexican war, in which is included any honorable mention made of Illinois soldiers as shown by excerpts from the official reports and orders of the various Generals under whom they served, so far as the same appear in the official reports of these officers to the War Department at Washington. It is of course not intended to give an extended view of the operations of the war, therefore our memoranda is scrupulously confined to the actual service of our volunteers, and presents only such data as has been derived from official and other reliable sources, which is considered necessary to make intelligible the official rosters, and which we hope, when taken in connection with them, will make an enduring and reliable memorial of their services, thus more than fulfilling the wish of the General Assembly, who have neither appropriated for, nor expected the publication of, little else than the records as received from the War Department. Although this publication as it now stands is incomplete, particularly in the matter of the records of service in the Winnebago war, and the first campaign of the Black Hawk war, every effort has been made to obtain the desired information, both by correspondence with individuals and the War Department, and the work as presented gives the final result of the best efforts of this office to meet the expectations of the General Assembly.

HISTORICAL MEMORANDA.

THE BLACK HAWK WAR.

The rolls furnished from the War Department, and published in this volume, although by no means complete, show that the State of Illinois furnished one hundred and seventy-four companies of volunteer rangers and spies, which were actually mustered into the service of the United States for various periods of time, during the Black Hawk War. This, of course, does not include large numbers of the State militia, who were under arms, and performed services of greater or less importance, and whose names will remain forever unknown, many of whom were never actually mustered by any United States military officer, nor have any rolls or other account of their service been preserved.

That the public may understand the service of these companies, and the part performed by them in that most important, of any of the Indian wars of the West, we will give a brief sketch of the causes which led to, and the principal events which occurred in, the Black Hawk War. The causes which led to that war reach back to, and even before, the Winnebago or Sauk War of 1827, and are, as briefly stated by Edwards, in his History of Illinois, as follows:

"During Gov. Edwards' administration, as Executive of the State, the Indians upon the Northwestern frontier began to be very troublesome. The different tribes not only commenced a warfare among themselves, in regard to their respective boundaries, but they extended their hostilities to the white settlements. A treaty of peace, in which the whites acted more as mediators than as a party, had been signed at Prairie du Chien, on the 19th day of August, 1825, by the terms of which the boundaries between the Winnebagoes and Sioux, Chippewas, Sauks, Foxes, and other tribes were defined, but it failed to keep them quiet. Their depredations and murders continued frequent, and in the summer of 1827 their conduct, particularly that of the Winnebagoes, became very alarming.

There is no doubt, however, that the whites, who at this period were immigrating in large numbers to the Northwest, and earnestly desired their removal further westward, purposely exasperated the Indians, at the same time that they greatly exaggerated the hostilities committed."—(Edwards' Hist. p. 218.)

A combination was soon formed by the different tribes of Indians under Red Bird, a chief of the Sioux, to kill or drive off all the whites above Rock river. This league, which included the Winnebagoes, Pottawotamies, and other tribes of the Northwest, commenced their offensive operations by killing two white men in the vicinity of Prairie du Chien, on the 24th day of July, 1827, and on the 30th of the same month they attacked two returning keel boats which had, on their upward trip, conveyed military stores to Fort Snelling, killing two of the crew and wounding four others, before they were repulsed. Governor Edwards, anticipating trouble, had, on the 14th day of July, issued an order to the commandants in Gen. Hanson's brigade, (located on the east side of the Illinois river), to detach one-fourth of their respective regiments, and be ready to meet any attack made by the Indians. On the same day he wrote to Col. Thomas M. Neale, of the Twentieth Regiment (from Sangamon county), to accept six hundred volunteers, who were to equip themselves, find their own subsistence, and continue in service thirty days, unless sooner discharged; to rendezvous the same at Fort Clark, and march with all possible expedition from there to Galena, to the assistance of the whites, as the Indians had threatened the settlers at the lead mines, near that place. The possession of these mines by the whites had always excited the serious jealousy of the Indians.

Under this call Col. Neale recruited one cavalry company, which was commanded by Capt. Edward Mitchell, and four companies of Infantry, commanded, respectively, by Captains Thomas Constant, Reuben Brown, Achilles Morris and Bowlin Green. The whole force under command of Col. Neale, (the other field officers are unknown except James D. Henry—Sheriff at the time of Sangamon County—Adjutant,) marched to Peoria, where the regiment was more fully organized, and from thence to Galena. Before their arrival, however, in the Indian country Red Bird and six of his principal warriors had surrendered, and the campaign being ended the volunteers returned to their homes. No rolls of these companies have been obtained, and if they were mustered into the United States service at all, the rolls were either never returned to the department, or have been mislaid.

While Col. Neale was recruiting and marching his regiment to Galena, the settlers there were not idle. A committee of safety had been formed and temporary defences were erected, and in pursuance of an order from Governor Edwards the miners were formed into companies and equipped for action, (the rolls of only one company of these militia have been furnished us, Capt. James M. Strode's, page 187.) These militia were placed under the immediate command of Gen. Henry Dodge, and formed an auxiliary force to the command of Brig.-Gen. Henry Atkinson, U. S. A., whose force consisted of six hundred regulars. Before the arrival of Col. Neale, these forces combining under Gen. Atkinson, marched into the Winnebago country and captured Red Bird, who, it appears by a letter of Gen. Street to Governor Edwards, voluntarily surrendered himself to the whites, coming into camp displaying a white flag. With Red Bird there also surrendered themselves six other Indians, including Black Hawk, who had not yet become famous. These Indians were retained in captivity several months, Red Bird dying during confinement; and some of them having been tried and convicted of complicity in the murder of white settlers, were executed on the 26th day of December, 1827. Black Hawk, against whom nothing could be proven, was acquitted, but it is alleged afterwards acknowledged his guilt and boasted of his connection with the murders for which he had been tried. With the death of Red Bird ended the Winnebago war. The tribe seemed to be thoroughly humbled by the result of the campaign, and although fears of further hostilities from them were for some time after entertained, they continued peaceable. In regard to the lands about which the difficulty originated, until the question of ownership could be adjusted amicably, they promised to keep away from the mines entirely, Gen. Atkinson promising them that "the next summer persons would come from their Great Father to consult with them about the matter."

"A talk was subsequently had with them in which they abandoned all the country south of the Wisconsin river. After this there was a general peace with the Indians throughout the western frontier." (Edwards' His. p. 224). In the meantime Governor Edwards did not cease his efforts to urge on the War Department the necessity of the entire removal of the Indians from the State, their presence being a constant menace, and their continued residence on lands which they had ceded being dangerous to the peace of the white settlers, who were constantly increasing in numbers, and whose animals the Indians did not hesitate to appropriate whenever opportunity offered. In October the Secretary of War informed the Governor that Governor Cass had been instructed to "take measures with regard to the removal of the Indians." But delays having occurred, and the Indians still remaining, on the 25th day of May, 1828, Governor Edwards wrote to Gen. Clark urging immediate action on the part of the Government. This he followed by a letter addressed to the Secretary of War, dated June 17th, in which he stated: "This grievance still continuing, and aggravated as it is by recent occurrences of which I am bound to presume you are informed, I feel it my duty to ask you what further in regard to this matter may be expected from the General Government." (Edwards' Hist. p. 226.)

Upon the urgent request of the Indians, and notwithstanding the earnest protest of the Governor (Edwards), twelve months additional time was given them in which to remove from the State. With regard to this delay and in a spirit of protest against the action of the Government in the premises, Governor Edwards wrote Gen. Clark, Indian agent at St. Louis, a letter, in the conclusion of which he used the following significant language: "If any act of hostility shall be committed on the frontiers, I will not hesitate to remove them on my own responsibility as Governor of the State." (Edwards' History, p. 227.)

As to the subsequent history of the causes which finally led to this outbreak, Edwards says:

About this time (1829) the President issued his proclamation, according to law, and, in pursuance thereof, all the country above the mouth of Rock river (the ancient seat of the Sauk nation) was sold to American families, and in the year following it was taken possession of by them. To avoid difficulty with the tribes another treaty, confirming previous ones, was made with the Sacs and Foxes, on the 15th of July, 1830, by the provisions of which they were to remove peacefully from the Illinois country. A portion of the Sacs, with their principal chief, Keokuk, at their head, quietly retired across the Mississippi. With those who remained in the village, at the mouth of Rock river, an arrangement was made by the Americans who had purchased the land, by which they were to live together as neighbors, the Indians still cultivating their old fields as formerly. Black Hawk, however, a restless and uneasy spirit, who had ceased to recognize Keokuk as chief, and who was known to be still under the pay of the British, emphatically refused either to remove from the lands or to respect the rights of the Americans to them. He insisted that Keokuk had no authority for making such a treaty, and he proceeded to gather around him a large number of the warriors and young men of the tribe, who were anxious to distinguish themselves as "braves," and, placing himself at their head, he determined to dispute with the whites the possession of the ancient seat of his nation. He had conceived the gigantic scheme, as appears by his own admissions, of uniting all the Indians, from the Rock river to the Gulf of Mexico, in a war against the United States, and he made use of every pretext for gaining accessions to his party.

In the meantime, on the 9th day of December, 1830, Hon. John Reynolds had been elected Governor of the State.

In pursuance of his declared intention of regaining possession of the ancient hunting grounds and the principal village of his tribe, in the month of April, 1831, Black Hawk recrossed the river, at the head of a force variously estimated at from three to five hundred braves of his own tribe, with from one to two hundred allies of the Pottawotamies and Kickapoos, bringing with them his women and children, with the avowed purpose of remaining.

Black Hawk immediately notified the whites that they must depart from the village, and they refusing to comply, their property was destroyed, and they suffered in person various indignities at the hands of the Indians. On the 30th of April, forty of these settlers sent a petition to Governor Reynolds, setting forth their grievances, and asking relief. Governor Reynolds, thus informed of the state of affairs, and believing that Black Hawk and his band were determined to retain possession of the country by force, resolved to effect their expulsion. A call was therefore made for volunteers (May 27, 1831,) and when it became known, the whole northwestern part of the State resounded to the clamor of war. No county south of St. Clair nor east of Sangamon was included in the call, which was limited to seven hundred men, who were to report within fifteen days' time, mounted and equipped, at the place of rendezvous, which was fixed at Beardstown, on the Illinois river. More than twice the number of men called for responded, and the Governor, finding so many willing and ready to go, decided to accept the services of the whole 1,600 men. They were moved to a camp two miles north of Rushville, and there organized into two regiments, and two battalions. One of the regiments elected James D. Henry, of Sangamon county, Colonel,* and the other elected Daniel Lieb, while Major Nathaniel Buckmaster was elected to command the "Odd Battalion." Major Samuel Whitesides was appointed by the Governor to the command of the "Spy Battalion," and the whole brigade was placed under the command of Hon. Joseph Duncan, then the member in Congress, and afterward Governor of the State, who was commissioned by Governor Reynolds as Brigadier General of militia. Colonels Enoch C. March and Samuel C. Christy were appointed quartermasters, while the Governor himself accompanied the expedition in his capacity of Commander-in-Chief of the militia of the State. They immediately (June 15th, 1831,) took up their march from camp near Rushville to Rock river, where they arrived on the 25th of June. Six companies of regular troops, which had been dispatched from Jefferson Barracks, under the command of Gen. Gaines, had arrived at Fort Armstrong a few days before, and had already had an unsatisfactory conference with Black Hawk, who declined to return across the river. Gen. Gaines met Governor Reynolds and his force at their encampment on the Mississippi, eight miles below the old Sac village, and after receiving the volunteers into the United States service, Gens. Gaines and Duncan concerted measures of attack. But the wily Black Hawk,

---

*Jacob Fry was Lieutenant-Colonel, and John T. Stuart Major.

no doubt well apprised of the number of the force which was ready to attack him, concluded not to risk an engagement, but on the night of the 25th had quietly recrossed the river, leaving his deserted camp and village to be peaceably taken possession of by the forces of the opposing Generals on the following morning. Out of vengeance, no doubt, for their disappointment at the escape of the Indians, and to remove future cause of dispute, the soldiers destroyed the village entirely by fire. As Governor Ford says in his history, "Thus perished this ancient village, which had been the delightful home of 6,000 to 7,000 Indians, where generation after generation had been born, had died and been buried." Gen. Gaines sent an order to Black Hawk requiring him and his band to return and enter into a treaty. They refusing to respond to the first invitation, a second and more peremptory mandate had the desired effect, and on the 30th day of June, 1831, Black Hawk and about thirty chiefs of the Sacs came, and in full council with Governor Reynolds and Gen. Gaines, signed an agreement, in which they agreed, among other things, that "no one or more shall ever be permitted to recross said river, to the usual place of residence, nor any part of their old hunting grounds east of the Mississippi, without permission of the President of the United States, or the Governor of the State of Illinois." The volunteer troops were then disbanded, and returned to their homes, while the subsistence gathered for their sustenance, was from time to time given by Gen. Gaines and the kind-hearted Governor to the Indians, who had, by their foolish invasion, rendered it impossible to raise any crop for that season, it being too late to plant any crop after the war had closed. Thus ended without bloodshed the first campaign of the Black Hawk war. Of the forces engaged therein, there are but the rolls of two companies, published herein. Capt. Solomon Miller's, from St. Clair county, and Capt. William Moore's, of the same county, both in Maj. Buckmaster's "Odd Battalion," (See pages 188, 190.)

1832—SECOND CAMPAIGN.

Notwithstanding the treaty, the trouble was not yet ended. In the spring of 1832 Black Hawk recrossed the Mississippi (April 6th) and commenced his march up Rock River Valley, accompanied by about five hundred warriors on horseback, while his women and children went up the river in their canoes. Gen. Atkinson, then stationed at Fort Armstrong, warned him against this aggression and ordered him to return, but this they refused to do, and went forward to the country of the Winnebagoes, with whom Black Hawk made arrangements to make a crop of corn, which reason he alleged to be the cause of the expedition. The Winnebagoes and Pottawotamies, however, both refused to yield to his solicitations to join him in a war against the whites.

On being informed of the movements of Black Hawk, Governor Reynolds (April 16th) called for a thousand mounted volunteers, from the central and southern parts of the State, to rendezvous at Beardstown, on the 22d of the same month. Daily accounts of the operations of the Indians were received. Judge Young, Col. Strode and Benjamin Mills wrote the Governor, urging speedy protection of the frontiers, as the inhabitants were in great danger. On receipt of this intelligence two hundred men (see pp. 151-4), under Major Stillman, were ordered to guard the frontier near the Mississippi, and two hundred (see Col. Johnson's regiment), under Major Bailey, the frontier between the Mississippi and the settlements on the Illinois. Such was the threatening aspect of affairs, that the call was extended to every part of the State. In the meantime eighteen hundred men had met at Beardstown, and were organized into a brigade of four regiments and an "odd" and a "spy" battalion. An election (April 28) for field officers, resulted in the election of Col. John Thomas to command the First Regiment, Col. Jacob Fry the Second Regiment, Col. Abram B. DeWitt the Third Regiment, Col. Samuel M. Thompson the Fourth Regiment* (in this regiment was Capt. Abraham Lincoln's† company—p. 10.), while Major James D. Henry, of Sangamon county, was elected to command the Spy Battalion (p. 106), in which Captains John Dawson, Thomas Carlin and John Dement commanded the companies, and Major Thomas James to the command of the "Odd" Battalion (page 110). A part of the "Odd" Battalion under Maj. Long, consisting of the companies commanded by Capt. Jacob Eby and Capt. Japhet A. Ball, both from Sangamon county, was "detached for foot purposes." Eight companies, not attached to any regiment (pp. 116-122), also served in this brigade. Governor Reynolds, who also accompanied the expedition, placed Brigadier-Gen. Whiteside in the immediate command, while Cols. March and Christy, the efficient quartermasters in the campaign of 1831, were relied on to gather the supplies for the present campaign. William Thomas was appointed Brigade Quartermaster, while Capts. James B. Stapp and Joseph M. Chadwick were appointed to the general staff. Maj. James Turney, paymaster; Vital Jarrot, of St. Clair county, adjutant general, and Cyrus Edwards, ordnance officer, were appointed to their positions on the staff of the Commander-in-Chief.

On the 29th day of April, the army left camp near Beardstown and marched to the Mississippi river, at or near the present town

---

*George Carpenter, Esq., of Springfield, furnishes to us the commission of his father, the late Major Carpenter, as paymaster of this regiment, a copy of which we give:

"I do hereby certify that William Carpenter is duly appointed Paymaster in the Fourth Regiment on the detachment of mounted volunteers, called into the service of the United States. He is therefore required diligently and carefully to discharge the duties of said office. Given under my hand this 30th day of April, 1832.
"SAMUEL M. THOMPSON, Colonel Fourth Regiment Volunteers."

†William L. Wilson, who was a private in Capt. M. G. Wilson's company, of Thompson's regiment, of Whiteside's brigade, writes to this office from Rushville, under date of February 3, 1882, and after detailing some interesting reminiscences of Stillman's defeat, says: "I have during that time had much fun with the afterwards President of the United States, Abraham Lincoln. I remember one time of wrestling with him, two best in three, and ditched him. He was not satisfied, and we tried it in a foot-race, for a five dollar bill. I won the money and 'tis spent long ago. And many more reminiscences could I give, but am of the Quaker persuasion and not much given to writing."

The following discharge paper was found among the papers of the late Col. Wm. Carpenter, formerly Paymaster of Col. Thompson's regiment. The blank was filled in the handwriting of Capt. Lincoln:

"I certify that Lewis W. Farmer volunteered and served as a private in the company of mounted volunteers under my command, in the regiment commanded by Col. Samuel M. Thompson, in the brigade under the command of Gens. S. Whiteside and H. Atkinson, called into the service of the United States by the Commander-in-Chief of the militia of the State, for the protection of the northwestern frontier against the invasion of the British band of Sac and other tribes of Indians; that he was enrolled on the 21st day of April, 1832, and was *honorably discharged* on the 7th day of June thereafter, having served forty-eight days. Given under my hand, this 21st day of September, 1832.
A. LINCOLN, Captain."

of Oquawka. On arriving at that place, and some delay occurring in the receipt of supplies, messengers were dispatched to Gen. Atkinson, at Fort Armstrong, who sent a boat loaded with provisions to the troops.

From here they marched up the river to the mouth of Rock river, where they were all received into the United States service by Gen. Atkinson. From this point the commanding general proceeded up the Rock river on a steamer, accompanied by a force of 400 regulars and an armament of cannon, while the volunteers under Gen. Whiteside marched through the swamps in the vicinity of the stream. They moved up Rock river without encountering savages until they arrived at the town of Dixon, on the evening of the 10th of May, where they found Majors Stillman and Bailey, who were at this place with their forces, where they had been directed to remain in their duty of protecting the frontier. Gen. Atkinson then sent out a scouting party of five men to confer with the chiefs of the Pottawotamies, and who, after getting lost, returned the third day afterward, reporting to have fallen in with some of Black Hawk's men who were encamped on a small stream known as Old Man's Creek, twelve miles above Dixon. Majors Stillman and Bailey having done but little service, besought the Governor to grant them the privilege of reconnoitering the enemy. Thereupon Governor Reynolds issued to them the following order: "Major Stillman: You will cause the troops under your immediate command, and the battalion under Major Bailey, to proceed without delay to the head of Old Man's Creek, where it is supposed there are some hostile Indians and coerce them into submission." On the following morning, May 14, 1832,) they started with 275 men (Stillman's Brigade. See page 151, for rolls of Bailey's command, afterward Fifth Regiment, pp. 102-5), and reached the Old Man's Creek without adventure, pursuing their course up that stream some fifteen miles, to Sycamore Creek. They dismounted for the purpose of passing the night. While engaged in camp duties, three Indians, bearing a white flag, came into camp, and were taken into custody. These

---

* From a memoranda kept by Major William Carpenter, paymaster of the Fourth regiment on this expedition, we subjoin the following as the distances marched by that command between different camps:

To Beardstown			50 miles.
" 1st camp	over Illinois river		9 "
" 2d "	Rushville		3 "
" 3d "	Crooked Creek		25 "
" 4th "	"		20 "
" 5th "	Yellow Banks		18 "
" 6th "	Camp Creek		30 "
" 7th "	Rock River		20 "
" 8th "	Cut bee tree		26 "
" 9th "	Timber scarce, man shot himself		30 "
" 10th "	Dixon		8 "
" 11th "	Battle ground (Stillman's defeat)		25 "
" 12th "	Return to Dixon's		25 "
" 13th "	Express came to us about the murder		12 "
" 14th "	Rock River—Capt. Gooden arrested		4 "
" 15th "	One mile to good spring traveled		16 "
" 16th "	Tishwakee		10 "
" 17th "	Sycamore, here the scalps were trimmed		12 "
" 18th "	Fox river timber		25 "
" 19th "	Six miles from Paw-paw		20 "
" 20th "	Two miles from the mouth of the river		20 "
	Then home in company with William Constant		110 "
	Total miles traveled		518

—2

were soon followed by five more, who came near the camp, no doubt with the purpose of inviting an attack. In this they succeeded, and a party of Stillman's men immediately started in pursuit, while others followed as soon as they could mount, and soon three-fourths of the command had joined in an irregular chase across the prairie. The soldiers overtook and killed two of the Indians, and pursued the others to the edge of the forest. At this juncture Black Hawk, with about forty of his men, arose from an ambush, and with terrific yells charged on the assailants, who, in their turn, retreated in hot haste, followed by the infuriated savages. The fearful din caused by the retreating soldiers and their pursuers caused a stampede in the remainder of the force of the camp, and they all fled, in an inglorious panic, and in spite of the efforts of Major Stillman and others to rally them, the retreat was continued until they all reached the main force at Dixon. Major Perkins and Captain Adams, of Tazewell County, with about fifteen men, made a stand in which they somewhat checked the Indians, and thus saved the lives of many of the fugitives, who would otherwise have fallen victims to their pursuers. This rally cost the brave Adams his life, his body being found the next day near the dead bodies of two of the savages, whom he had undoubtedly slain before he himself was killed. As a result of the fight, eleven whites and seven Indians were killed, besides many wounded on both sides.

During the night of the battle, known since as "Stillman's Run," Governor Reynolds made a requisition for 2,000 men to be in readiness for future operations, while the utmost consternation spread throughout the State and Nation. Exaggerated reports of the numbers of the Indians, and the skill, ability, cunning and cruelty of Black Hawk, added much to the general alarm.

General Scott, with 1,000 United States troops, was immediately ordered to the Northwest, to superintend the future operations of the campaign.

When the news of Stillman's defeat reached the camp at Dixon, a council of war was held, and it was determined to return immediately to the battle field.

The next morning, after obtaining ten oxen from Col. John Dixon, which were slaughtered and issued to the men, without bread or salt, the whole force marched to the scene of the encounter. The dead were recovered, in most instances frightfully mutilated, and the fragments gathered together and buried; but although Major Henry and his men effectually scoured the surrounding country for miles in every direction, the enemy could not be found, and the whole force fell back to Dixon.

The new levies, under the call of Gov. Reynolds, were to meet, some on the 3d of June, at Beardstown, and the others on the 10th of the same month at Hennepin.

The men first recruited, now asked to be discharged, but the Governor appealing to their patriotism, they agreed to remain from 12 to 15 days longer, and the companies under Bailey (Covell's, McClure's, Pugh's and Adams'), with Stillman's battalion, (Captains Eads', Barnes' and Ball's companies) were organized into a regiment, known as the Fifth Regiment of Whiteside's Brigade, under Colonel James Johnson, and received into the service of the United

States, and one part ordered to Ottawa, for the defense of that place, while the other remained at Dixon to guard the stores, around which General Atkinson had caused embankments to be thrown.

On the 19th of May the whole army marched up the river in pursuit of the enemy, and on the evening of the same day received news of the massacre of several whites on Indian Creek, not far from Ottawa.

General Atkinson ordered Gen. Whitesde's and Col. Taylor (afterwards President of the United States) to continue the pursuit with the volunteers, while he, with the regulars, returned to Dixon. After following trails in several directions, which proved that the Indians had divided and left the immediate country for the north, and the troops expressing a determination to return to their homes, were brought to the mouth of Rock River, and there discharged on the 27th and 28th days of May, and thus the campaign ended without effecting any important results.

SECOND CAMPAIGN— 1832.

On the requisition of Gen. Atkinson, the Governor called for 1,000 additional men, which were recruited out of the disbanded men for immediate service, for a term of twenty days, until the new levies should arrive. This regiment, which was filled without difficulty, organized by the election of Jacob Fry, as Colonel; James D. Henry, as Lieutenant-Colonel.

Although this regiment does not appear grouped together, as it should be, in this record, the companies, as well as can now be ascertained, were Capt. Samuel Smith's company (page 168), Capt. B. James' company (page 169), Capt. Elijah Iles' company (page 174) —(This company contained *private*

ABRAHAM LINCOLN,

who had been that day mustered out, with his company, as a captain, and reënlisted with many of his men in Capt. Iles' company, for this emergency service)—Capt. Alex. D. Cox's company (page 178), Capt. Wm. C. Ball's company (182), Capt. Alexander White's company (page 183), and Capt. A. W. Snyder's company (page 185). This regiment, after bravely guarding the imperiled frontier, was mustered out of the service on the 15th day of June, except Capt. Iles' company, which was discharged the 16th, and Capt. Snyder's discharged the 21st of June. This latter company had some severe skirmishing with the enemy, some seventy in number, near Kellogg's Grove, in which four of the Indians and two of the whites were killed.

On the 6th of June, Black Hawk, with about 150 warriors, made an attack on Apple River Fort, situated a quarter of a mile north of the present village of Elizabeth and twelve miles from Galena. Three messengers, on their way from Dixon to Galena, were fired upon when one-half mile from the fort, and one of them wounded, but all of them escaped to the fort. The inhabitants, alarmed at the shots, fled to the fort, which was invested, and a continual fire kept up for fifteen hours by the savages, who had taken possession of the dwellings of the whites, from which they fired through holes made for that purpose through the walls. The twenty-five men composing the garrison, made such a determined resistance that the savages, after having destroyed everything within their reach, departed, taking with them all the stock, provisions and movable property of the settlers. Only one man of the whites was killed, while the loss of the savages has never been ascertained. Col. Strode, of the militia, arrived the next day from Dixon with a force to their relief, but the enemy had made good his escape.

The savages having attacked and killed two men near Ft. Hamilton, five miles from Galena, Gen. Dodge, of Wisconsin, followed them, with the force under his command, and, overtaking them at Pecatonica, charged upon them and killed the whole number, with a loss of three men killed in his own force.

Capt. Stephenson, of Galena, and a part of his company, had a little skirmish with the enemy between Apple River Fort and Kellogg's Grove, and were repulsed by the Indians, who had taken shelter in a small grove, with the loss of three killed and the Captain and several others seriously wounded.

The new levies met as provided in the call, at Beardstown and Hennepin, but were afterward ordered to Fort Wilbourne, a small fortification on the south bank of the Illinois river, about a mile above Peru, which had been erected by Lieut. Wilbourne for the protection of the stores entrusted to his care by Col. March.

A promiscuous multitude of several thousands had assembled, among them many of the most prominent men in the State, and the selection of officers was a matter requiring great delicacy and tact. But after the organization of the companies, the captains of the several companies and the Governor agreed that the principal officers should be determined by an election, in which all the troops should participate. The brigades were organized, and on the 16th day of June Alexander Posey was elected General of the First, Milton K. Alexander of the Second, and James D. Henry of the Third. Gen. Atkinson received them into the service of the United States, and took the general command of the force thus organized, which amounted to 3192 men.

The Governor appointed to his staff, as Aids, Benjamin F. Hickman and Alex. F. Grant, James Turney, Adjutant General, and Col. E. C. March, Q. M. General. Besides the main army four battalions were organized for special purposes, commanded severally by Majors Bogart and Bailey, and Colonels Buckmaster and Dement.

The brigades were composed of three regiments each, commanded by officers of their own selection, but no rolls of the regimental field and staff, nor of the staff of the different brigade commanders are in the possession of this office, though supposed to exist among the records of the War Department at Washington, D. C.

In view of the disasters which threatened the northern frontier, the Governor ordered a chain of forts to be erected from the Mississippi to Chicago.

On the 17th day of June, Col. Dement, with his spy battalion of 150 men, was ordered to report himself to Col. Taylor at Dixon, while the main army was to follow. On his arrival at Dixon he was ordered to take position in Kellogg's grove, where, on the 25th day of June, he was visited by Mr. Funk, of McLean County, who, while on his way from the lead mines the night before, reported that a trail of about 300 Indians leading northward had been seen that day. A council of war, held that night, determined that Col. Dement and fifty picked men should reconnoiter the surrounding country the next day. At daylight the party sallied forth, and when within 300 yards of the fort discovered several Indian spies. Regardless of the cries of Col. Dement and Lieut.-Governor Casey, who accompanied him, and without waiting for direction, these undrilled and undisciplined men immediately charged on the foes, and recklessly following them, despite all efforts of Col. Dement to check them, were led into an ambush, and suddenly were confronted by 300 howling, naked savages under the command of Black Hawk in person. The sudden appearance of the savages created a panic among the whites, and each man struck out for himself in the direction of the fort, with a speed which equalled, if it did not excel, the alacrity with which they left it in the morning.

In the confused retreat which followed, five of the whites, who were without horses, were killed, while the remainder reached the fort, and dismounting, entered it, closely pursued by the enemy. The fort was vigorously assailed for over an hour by the savages, who were repulsed, and forced to retire, leaving nine of their number behind them, dead on the field, besides several others carried away wounded. No one in the fort was killed, but several wounded. Col. Dement received three shots through his clothing, but fortunately escaped unhurt. At 8 o'clock in the morning, messengers were sent fifty miles to Gen. Posey for assistance, and towards sundown that General and his brigade made their appearance, and no further attack was made on the fort by the savages. Gen. Posey started out in search of the enemy the next day, but the trail showed that they had pursued their favorite tactics of scattering their forces, and the pursuit was abandoned. The army continued its march up Rock river, near the source of which they expected to find the enemy. As provisions were scarce and difficult to convey for any distance, the command of Gen. Alexander, with a detachment under Gen. Henry and Maj. Dodge, was sent to Fort Winnebago, between Fox and Wisconsin rivers, to obtain supplies. Learning that Black Hawk was encamped on the Whitewater, Gen. Henry and Maj. Dodge started in immediate pursuit, leaving Gen. Alexander with his command in charge of the provisions to return to Gen. Atkinson. After several days' hard marches, and much suffering from exposure and lack of food, on the 21st day of July, the enemy were overtaken on the bluffs of the Wisconsin, and a decisive battle fought, in which Gen. Henry commanded the American forces, which consisted of Maj. Dodge's battalion on the right, Col. Jones, regiment in the center, and Col. Collins' on the left, with Maj. Ewing's battalion in the front, and Col. Fry's regiment in the rear as a reserve force. In this order they charged the enemy, and drove him from position after position with great loss, till the sun went down, leaving them victors, in the first important advantage gained over the enemy during the war.

In the morning it was discovered that the Indians had fled in the direction of the Mississippi river, leaving 168 dead on the field, and of their wounded, taken with them, twenty-five were found dead the next day on their trail, while Gen. Henry lost only one man killed and eight wounded. Litters were constructed for the wounded, and on the 23d of July, the army was again in motion, and after some difficulty on account of high water, reached Blue Mounds in safety. where they met Gen. Atkinson with the regulars, and the balance of the volunteer force. A return of the force at this time showed in Posey's brigade 200 effective men, Alexander's 850, in Henry's 300, while the regulars under Gen. Brady mustered 400 men; all told, the force mustered about 1,200 effective men,—though much reduced since the beginning of the campaign, still more than twice the number possessed by Black Hawk when in his best state of preparation, before any of the fights.

On the 25th the whole army was again put in motion, to try to find the Indians. Having spent two days in crossing the Wisconsin river, near Helena, on the 28th they came up with the trail of the Indians, the abandoned articles, and dead bodies strewed along the trail, showing them to be in a deplorable condition, and suffering for food. On the morning of the 2nd of August, the army reached the bluffs of the Mississippi, some distance, however, from the stream. The Indians had reached the river, and were making active preparations to cross. Some had already crossed, and some of the women and children had started down the river in canoes to Prairie du Chien, which they afterward reached in a starving condition. In this condition the Indians, when they arrived at the river, were attacked by a force under Capt. Throckmorton, who was on the steamer Warrior, and who, with a six-pound cannon, loaded with canister, destroyed many of the luckless fugitives, although they had displayed a white flag, which he refused to recognize. The fuel in the steamer having failed, it fell down the river to Prairie du Chien. Although he had killed twenty-three Indians and wounded many more, Capt. Throckmorton intended to return after wooding up, and finish the remainder. Before he could execute his intention, however, Gen. Atkinson had fallen on the unfortunate savages where they were encamped, at the mouth of the Bad Axe, a creek emptying into the Mississippi river, and had commenced a general battle, in which the Indians were completely routed, and suffered a loss of 150 killed, besides many drowned, and many more wounded. A large number of women and children lost their lives, owing to the fact that it was impossible to distinguish them from the men. [Davidson and Stuvé's Hist. 405.] The American loss was seventeen killed.

This battle virtually ended the war. Gen. Atkinson, with his whole force, and prisoners, [about fifty women and children], fell down the river to Prairie du Chien. On the 7th day of August, Gen. Winfield Scott, who, with nine companies of infantry, had been sent from Fortress Monroe, arrived, and assumed command. He had arrived with four of these companies at Chicago the day before, making the march of 1,800 miles in eighteen days, part of the way by steamer on the lakes, having left behind three companies, who had contracted Asiatic cholera at Detroit, at Fort Gratiot, forty miles from that city. This disease preyed to such an extent on the forces who came through, that they remained in Chicago until the latter part of the month before coming on to Fort Armstrong, their final destination. The volunteers now returned to Dixon, and were discharged on the 17th day of August. On the 27th Black Hawk, having been captured by some treacherous Winnebagoes, was delivered to the whites at Prairie du Chien, and he and his family were sent as hostages to Fortress Monroe, and there retained until June, 1833. In September, 1832, a treaty was made which ended the Indian troubles in this State, and although a few companies were detained a few weeks longer, the main body of the force returned to their homes in August, 1832.

Black Hawk, upon regaining his liberty, ever after conducted himself in a friendly manner to the whites. In 1837 he again visited Washington with a deputation of the chiefs of his tribe, on the invitation of the President, to settle differences which had occasioned a violent war with them and the Sioux. After his return he settled in what is now known as Lee county, Iowa. In the spring of 1838 he built himself a dwelling on the Des Moines river, 20 miles above its mouth. In this he moved his family, and prepared to farm and live after the manner of the whites. On a visit made to Burlington, the following autumn, he took cold, which brought on a disease which terminated his eventful life, and at the age of 72 Black Hawk was gathered to his fathers.

Perhaps no one of his race ever excelled Black Hawk in patriotism or love for his country. He fought an unequal battle for the home and the graves of his ancestors. In his last speech to the Americans he said: "Rock River was a beautiful country. I like my towns, my cornfields and the home of my people. I fought for it. It is now yours. It will produce you good crops."

A dispassionate view of the war and its causes will show that he had grievances, and when he had failed to redress them in a peaceable manner, had resorted to arms, because he thought it the only possible arbitrament.

Besides the companies of Capt. Joseph Napier [page 149], Capt. Holden Session [page 148] and Capt. James Walker [page 178], the latter from Walker's Grove, now Plainfield Township, in Will county, all of which were recruited within the limits of the then county of Cook; another company was organized for home defense within the city of Chicago, a muster roll of which is preserved in a book entitled "Early Chicago," by Hon. John Wentworth, being the third paper published by that gentleman on the early history of the city of Chicago, (No. 16, Fergus Hist. Phamplets).

MUSTER ROLL.

May 3, 1832.—We, the undersigned, agree to submit ourselves, for the time being, to Gholson Kercheval, Captain, and George W. Dale and John S. C. Hogan, First and Second Lieutenants, as commanders of the militia of the town of Chicago, until all apprehension of danger from the Indians may have subsided:

Richard J. Hamilton,
Jesse B. Brown,
Isaac Harmon,
Samuel Miller,
John F. Herndon,
Benjamin Harris,
S. T. Gage,
Rufus Brown,
Jeremiah Smith,
Heman S. Bond,
William Smith,
Isaac D. Harmon,
Joseph Lafromboise,
Henry Boucha,
Claude Lafromboise,
J. W. Zarley,
David Wade,
William Bond,
Samuel Ellis.

Jeddiah Wooley,
George H. Walker,
A. W. Taylor,
James Kinzie,
David Pemeton,
James Ginsday,
Samuel Debaif,
John Wellmaker,
Wm. H. Adams,
James T. Osborne,
E. D. Harmon,
Charles Moselle,
Francis Labaque,
Michael Ouilmette,
Christopher Shedaker,
David McKee,
Ezra Bond,
Robert Thompson.

THE MEXICAN WAR.

The volunteers from the State of Illinois performed such a conspicuous part in the war with Mexico, that it is necessary to give an epitome of the war, to be able to understand and appreciate the nature and value of their services, and render them the due credit which their importance demands.

On the 11th day of May, 1846, Congress passed an act, declaring that "By the act of the Republic of Mexico, a state of war exists between that Government and the United States." At the same time that body made an appropriation of ten million dollars to carry on the war, and authorized the President to accept fifty thousand volunteers.

This force, for convenience sake, to save transportation, and because of their already well-known familiarity with fire-arms, was drawn principally from the Southern and Western States. Illinois was called on for three regiments of infantry or riflemen, and the pay, with all allowances, placed at $15.50 per month to the private soldier. The militia of the State being then in an unorganized condition, Governor Ford issued a call for thirty full companies of volunteers of a maximum of eighty men, to serve for twelve months, and with the privilege of electing their own company and regimental officers.

The response to the call was enthusiastic in the extreme. Within ten days thirty-five full companies had organized and reported. By the time the place of rendezvous had been selected, (Alton), there had been seventy-five companies recruited,—each furious to go—of which the Governor (Ford) was compelled to select thirty companies —the full quota of the State—and the forty-odd unsuccessful companies were doomed to the disappointment of remaining at home. Of these thirty companies, were organized the *First* Regiment, Col. *John J. Hardin;* the *Second* Regiment, *Col. William H. Bissell*, and the *Third* Regiment, *Col. Ferris Foreman*, which were recruited during the months of April, May and June, and mustered into the United States service, at Alton, Ill., on the 2d day of July, 1846.

Hon. E. D. Baker, then a member of Congress from the Capital district, induced the Secretary of War to accept another regiment from this State, and thereupon the *Fourth* Illinois was organized and mustered into the service on the 18th day of July, 1846, and served in the same brigade with the Third Regiment until both were discharged.

The First and *Second Regiments* must be considered together, as their history is the same.

These regiments were transported separately down the Mississippi River and across the Gulf, and re-joined each other on the first day of August at Camp Erwin, near the old town of Victoria, on Weuloop river, and after marching together to San Antonio, Texas, they joined General Wool's army of the center. They left that city on the 26th day of September. Marching steadily along, they entered Santa Rosa on the 24th day of October with no opposition. Thence they marched to Monclova, thence to Parras, where the original idea of the march, the capture of Chihuahua, was abandoned.

After remaining at this place twelve days, General Wool started to intercept, if possible, Santa Anna's attack on Monterey, and on the 21st of December occupied Agua Nueva, thus completing a six weeks' march of about one thousand miles, which had been barren of results. In January, 1847, General Taylor proceeded from Saltillo and formed a junction with Gen. Wool. On the 22d day of February, 1847, was begun the battle of Buena Vista, which ended on the 23d, and resulted in a complete victory for the American forces, and in which these two Illinois regiments covered themselves with glory.

Concerning the conduct of the Illinois volunteers at the battle of Buena Vista, we quote from an extended report made by Major General Zach. Taylor, U. S. A., commanding, dated

"AGUA NUEVA, March 6, 1847.

"The First and Second Illinois and the Second Kentucky Regiments served immediately under my eye, and I bear a willing testimony to their excellent conduct throughout the day. The spirit and gallantry with which the First Illinois and Second Kentucky engaged the enemy in the morning, restored confidence to that part of the field, while the list of casualties will show how much these three regiments suffered in sustaining the heavy charge of the enemy in the afternoon. Captain Conner's Company of Texas Volunteers attached to the Second Illinois Regiment, fought bravely, its Captain being wounded and two subalterns killed. Colonel Bissell, the only surviving Colonel of these regiments, merits notice for his coolness and bravery on this occasion. After the fall of the field officers of the First Illinois and Second Kentucky Regiments, the command of the former devolved upon Lieutenant Colonel Weatherford, and that of the latter upon Major Fry. Regimental commanders and others, who have rendered reports, speak in general terms of the good conduct of their officers and men, and have specified many names, but the limits of this report forbid a recapitulation of them here. I may, however, mention * * * Lieutenant Colonel Weatherford, First Illinois Regiment, Lieutenant Colonel Morrison, Major Trail and Adjutant Whiteside (severely wounded), Second Illinois Regiment, and Major Fry, Second Kentucky Regiment, as being favorably noticed for gallantry and good conduct. * * * To Major Warren, First Illinois Volunteers, I feel much indebted, for his firm and judicious course, while exercising command in the city of Saltillo." (MSS. and doc. 1847, p. 139.)

From a return of troops engaged in the action of the 22d and 23d day of February, A. D. 1847, made by General Zachery Taylor to the Adjutant General of the Army, under date of March 6th, we quote as follows:

FIRST ILLINOIS.

Eight companies—1 Colonel, 1 Lieutenant Colonel, 8 Captains, 1 Adjutant, 18 Subalterns, 519 non-commissioned officers and privates. Sick—Two commissioned officers and 25 non-commissioned officers and privates, making an aggregate of 580 officers and privates.

SECOND ILLINOIS.

Eight companies—1 Colonel, 1 Major, 7 Captains, 1 Adjutant, 19 Subalterns, 496 non-commissioned officers and privates. Sick—Four commissioned officers, 40 non-commissioned officers and privates. Aggregate, 573 officers and privates.

From an official return of the killed, wounded and missing in battle of Buena Vista, we quote:

FIRST ILLINOIS FOOT.

Killed—One Colonel, one Captain, one Subaltern, 26 enlisted men. Total, 26.

Wounded—Two Subalterns, 16 enlisted men, missing, 3. Aggregate loss, 47.

SECOND ILLINOIS FOOT.

Killed—Two Captains, one Subaltern, 29 enlisted men.

Wounded—Two Captains, six Subalterns, 63 enlisted men. Missing, four enlisted men. Aggregate loss, 126.

With the exception of the sending out of an occasional foraging detachment no further service was performed by these two regiments during the war. They remained at Buena Vista until the latter part of May, when the following order was issued:

HEADQUARTERS, BUENA VISTA,
May 28, 1847.

Orders No. 302.

The term of service for which the First and Second Illinois regiments have engaged to serve the United States has nearly expired, and they are about to return to their homes. The General commanding takes this occasion to express his deep regret at the departure of those who have been so long under his immediate command, and who have served so well their country.

Few can boast of longer marches, greater hardships, or more privations, and none of greater gallantry on the field of Buena Vista. It was there that the General witnessed with infinite satisfaction their valor, which gave additional luster to our arms, and increased glory to our country. To their steadiness and firmness in connection with the Second Kentucky regiment of foot, in resisting the Mexicans at a critical moment, and when there were five to one against them, and as General Santa Anna said, "where blood flowed in torrents and the field of battle was strewed with their dead," we may justly ascribe a large share of the glorious victory achieved over 20,000 men. A great victory it is true; but obtained at too great a sacrifice. Hardin, Zabriska, McKee, Woodward, Yell, Clay, and many others, fell leading their men to the charge. Their named and gallant deeds will ever be remembered by a grateful people. In taking leave of these regiments, the General cannot omit to express his admiration of the conduct and gallant bearing of all, and especially of Cols. Bissell and Weatherford and their officers, who have on all occasions done honor to themselves, and heroically sustained the cause of their country in the battle of Buena Vista. His best wishes will attend them to their homes, where they will be received with joy and gladness as the pride of their families and of their States.

By command of Brig.-Gen. WOOL.

IRWIN McDOWELL, Assistant Adjutant General.

These regiments were discharged at Camargo, Mexico, on the 17th day of June, 1847.

THE THIRD AND FOURTH REGIMENTS

were like the first two, brigaded together during their entire service. They were placed in Gen. Paterson's division, and marching from Matamoras to Tampico, formed part of Gen. Shields' force while he was in command of that city. On the 9th day of March, the Third and Fourth Regiments took part in the descent on Vera Cruz. Gen. Scott says in his report, dated Vera Cruz, March 14, 1847: "I could not postpone the descent, successfully made on the 9th inst., for half of the surf boats, Brig.-Gen. Shields' brigade, (old volunteers from Tampico), or the wagons and teams, which were then behind. That General landed with the army, having a small part of one of his old regiments, (three companies of the Third Illinois Foot), and the New York regiment of new volunteers." (Mess. and Doc. 1847, p. 218.) Gen. Scott was mistaken in attributing to the Third Illinois credit due to the Fourth. Though both regiments took part in the expedition, it was companies "A," "F" and "G," of the Fourth Illinois, under the immediate command of Lieut.-Col. John Moore, who made the landing referred to, Capt. H. A. Roberts, of Co. "A," from Sangamon county, being the first man to place his foot on the enemy's soil.

In the battle of Cerro Gordo, the Third and Fourth were hotly engaged, and gained great credit for their bravery. Gen. Scott, in his report of that battle to the Secretary of War, under date of April 23, 1847, says:

> Early on the morning of the 18th, the columns moved to the general attack, and our success was speedy and decisive. * * * The Brigade so gallantly led by Gen. Shields, and after his fall, by Col. Baker, deserves high commendation for its fine behavior and success. Cols. Foreman and Burnett, and Maj. Harris (Fourth Illinois) commanded the regiments; Lieut. Hammond, Third artillery, and Lieut. Davis, Illinois volunteers, constituted the brigade staff. (Mess. and Doc. 1847, p. 263.)

Brig.-Gen. Twiggs, who was in the immediate command of all the advanced forces, in a report to the General-in-Chief, dated April 19, 1847, (the day following the battle), says:

> Of the conduct of the volunteer force under the brave Gen. Shields, I cannot speak in too high terms. After he was wounded, portions of the three regiments were with me when I arrived first at the Jalapa road, and drove before them the enemy's cannoneers from their loaded guns. Their conduct and names shall be the subject of a special report. (Mess. and Doc. 1847, p. 276.)

From the report of Maj.-Gen. Patterson, commanding the volunteer division at the battle of Cerro Gordo, under date of April 23, 1847, and made to the commanding General, we extract:

> "On the afternoon of the 17th, a rapid and continuous fire of artillery and infantry, announcing that the Second division of regulars was closely engaged with the left of the enemy's lines, I was instructed, and immediately directed the Third volunteer brigade, under Brig.-Gen. Shields, to proceed at once to its support. Before the brigade reached the position of that division, the action had ceased for the day; the night was, however, occupied in establishing several pieces of artillery upon a height adjacent to the "Cerro Gordo."
>
> Early on the morning of the 18th the brigade moved to turn the extreme left of the enemy's line, resting on the Jalapa road. This was done over rugged ascents and through dense chapparal, under a severe and continuous flank fire from the enemy. Brig.-Gen. Shields, whilst gallantly leading his command, and forming it for the attack of the enemy, posted in force in his front, fell severely wounded, and was carried from the field.
>
> Col. Baker, Fourth Illinois regiment, having assumed the command, the enemy's lines were charged with spirit and success by the Third and Fourth Illinois, and the New York regiment, under the respective commanders, Cols. Foreman and Burnett, and Major Harris. The rout now becoming general, the brigade pressed forward in rapid pursuit, leaving a sufficient force to secure the artillery, specie, baggage, provisions and camp equipage left in our hands."

Later in same report Gen. Patterson says: "The attention of the general-in-chief is particularly called to the gallantry of Brig.-Gens. Pillow and Shields, who were both wounded at the head of their respective brigades; and to Col. Baker, who led Shields' brigade during a severe part of the action, and during the pursuit; and Lieut. G. T. M. Davis, Illinois volunteer aid-de-camp to Shields' brigade."

The loss of both regiments is given in the official reports of killed and wounded, forwarded to the War Department after the battle, as follows:

Third Illinois—Killed, 1; wounded, 15; total, 16.
Fourth Illinois—Killed, 5; wounded, 43; total, 48.

This office is in receipt of a letter dated February 5, 1882, from Second Lieut. W. A. Tinney, of the Fourth Illinois volunteers, in which he says: "We stormed their fort and put the enemy to flight, taking about six thousand prisoners, and we captured Gen. Santa Anna's carriage, also his wooden leg, which I have in my possession."

The Third and Fourth Regiments were shortly afterward returned by vessels to New Orleans, where they were discharged from the 23d to the 25th days of May, 1847.

THE FIFTH REGIMENT,

which is known officially as the First Regiment, Illinois Volunteers "during the war" (the other regiments having been enlisted for "twelve months"), was called out, under the requisition made by the Secretary of War April 19th, 1847, for six thousand more volunteers to "serve during the war," to take the place of those whose term of enlistment was to expire. Of this call, but one regiment was assigned to the State of Illinois, which was organized June 8th, 1847, at Alton, Illinois, by the election of E. W. B. Newby as Colonel.

This regiment left Alton by steamer, for Fort Leavenworth June 14, and from thence marched across the plains to Santa Fe. In October, 1847, the first battalion with a part of a Missouri regiment marched to El Paso. The other battalion remained at Santa Fe, as a garrison. This regiment lost heavily by sickness and exposure in its long marches across the plains, but was engaged in no battles or skirmishes with the enemy. It was mustered out of the service at Alton, Illinois, from the 15th to the 18th day of October, 1848.

THE SIXTH REGIMENT,

otherwise known as the Second Regiment, enlisted "during the war," was organized out of the overflow of companies which were raised for the Fifth Regiment.

So much honor had been achieved by the four regiments sent out by this State the first year of the war, that their praise was on every lip, and the young and ambitious were ready to make any sacrifice to be able to go and fight the Mexicans. When the call was made for the Fifth Regiment it was difficult again for the Governor to select, as the men poured in by hundreds, and enough reported in ten days time to fill half a dozen regiments. Application was again made to the Secretary of War by Lieutenant Colonel Hicks and others for leave to organize another regiment. It was hard to refuse these veterans of Buena Vista and Cerro Gordo, and the permission was granted, and the regiment was organized at Alton. Illinois, on the 3d day of August, 1847, by the election of J. Collins as Colonel.

Shortly after the regiment was mustered into the United States service it was forwarded by steamer to New Orleans, and there divided into two battalions. Companies A, D, E, F and H, under command of Colonel Collins, being sent to Vera Cruz, where they arrived on the 31st day of August, 1847. They were shortly afterwards engaged in a skirmish with the guerrillas, but saw no further actual service, save the duties of camp and garrison life. The Second Battalion, under Lieutenant Colonel Hicks, consisted of Companies B, C, G, I and K, and was forwarded by vessel to

Tampico and there performed garrison duty until discharged. Both battalions, as the muster rolls show, lost heavily from sickness, incident to the climate, as might have been expected of raw and unacclimated men in so dangerous a climate. This regiment was mustered out on the 20th to the 25th days of July, 1848, at Alton, Illinois.

INDEPENDENT MOUNTED VOLUNTEERS.

The rolls furnished this office from the war office in Washington show that four independent companies of cavalry were mustered into the United States service during the Mexican war. All enlisted the second year of the war, and mustered in, as all troops were, under the second call, for "during the war." Of these, the first recruited,

CAPT. ADAM DUNLAP'S COMPANY,

was recruited during the month of May, 1847, at Rushville, at Schuyler county, and was mustered into the United States service in Alton, on the 21st day of the same month, its enlistment being authorized by the same order under which Col. Newby's regiment was recruited. This company was never engaged in any actual battle, but did considerable scouting service, and was in several skirmishes with the guerrillas and scouts of the enemy. This company also lost heavily, as did all the volunteers of that year, by sickness, several men having died while at Matamoras. It was finally discharged at Alton, Illinois, on the 7th day of November, 1848, having served eighteen months in all, being distinguished as the longest term of service of any company from this State in the whole war.

CAPT. WYATT B. STAPP'S COMPANY.

This company was recruited at Monmouth, in the month of June, 1847, and was mustered in at Quincy, Illinois, on the 10th day of August, 1847. It lost severely by sickness at Perote and Jalapa, and was finally returned to the States, without adventure of serious nature, and was mustered out at Alton on the 26th day of July, 1848, lacking fifteen days of serving one year from the date of muster.

FIRST LIEUT. GEORGE C. LANPHERE,

Of this company, returned home in the spring of 1848, to recruit for his company, and during the months of March, April, and May had recruited thirty-one men [page 309], who were never sent to the company, but were mustered out by order of the Secretary of War, at Jefferson Barracks, near St. Louis, Mo., June 28, 1848.

CAPT. MICHAEL K. LAWLER'S COMPANY.

During the month of August, 1847, Capt. Lawler, who was a veteran of the Black Hawk War, recruited an independent company of cavalry at Shawneetown, which was mustered into the United

States service at place of enrollment, on August 18, and forwarded to Mexico via the New Orleans route. Except the common experiences with fever, reptiles and insects, this company had no encounter with foes of any kind, and after some routine service, laborious but unimportant, was returned to place of enlistment, and mustered out on the 26th day of October, 1848.

CAPT. JOSIAH LITTLE'S COMPANY

was conspicuous as the last company received into the United States service, being mustered in at Alton on the 11th day of September, 1847. No record of its service has been received, and we can only add that it was mustered out at the same place July 25, 1848.

"REGULAR" ENLISTMENTS FROM ILLINOIS.

On the 11th day of February, 1848, Congress passed an act authorizing the President to raise ten new regiments for the Regular Army to be enlisted for "during the war." These regiments were all recruited prior to the 30th of September of the same year, and consisted of a regiment of Voltigeurs, eight regiments of Infantry, the Ninth, Tenth, Eleventh, Twelfth, Thirteenth, Fourteenth, Fifteenth and Sixteenth, and the Third regiment of Dragoons. These regiments were recruited at various stations all over the United States. Of these regiments the Twelfth, Thirteenth and Fourteenth regiments were recruited by Brig.-Gen. G. M. Brooke, at New Orleans, while the Fifteenth and Sixteenth were recruited by Lieut. Col. J. Erving, at Cincinnati. As will appear by the rolls published, Illinois furnished two companies for the Sixteenth and one company for the Fourteenth regiment, under this call. As to the history of these regiments we find that the Fourteenth regiment was brigaded with the Voltigeur regiment and the Eleventh Infantry, and under Brig.-Gen. Cadwalader was engaged in the battle of El Molino del Rey, on the 8th day of September, 1847. Concerning their conduct Major Gen. Worth, in his official report of the engagement, made to the Commander-in-Chief, dated Tacayuba, September 10th, 1847, says:

"I desire to bring the notice of the General-In-Chief to the gallantry and good conduct of Brig.-Gen. Cadwalader and his command, by which the most timely and essential service was rendered in supporting the attack, and following up the success. Such movements as he was directed to make were executed with zeal and promptness." (Mess. and Doc. 1847, p. 366.)

From a return of killed and wounded in this engagement accompanying this report, it appears that the Fourteenth regiment lost, Killed—1 Corporal. Wounded—1 Field Officer, 1 Captain, 3 Lieutenants, 2 Corporals and 16 Privates.

No official report of the service of the Sixteenth regiment is in possession of this office or at present accessible.

By General Order No. 25, A. G. O., June 8, 1848, the enlisted men of these two regiments, as well as others enlisted under the same act, were ordered to be mustered out, the Fourteenth at New Orleans, and the Sixteenth at Newport Barracks, Kentucky, which was done accordingly.

As several recruiting stations were opened in the Southwestern States, quite a number of Illinois men were recruited in the Regular Army proper, notably in the Fourth regiment. A member of this regiment, Mr. J. W. Thomson, of Princeton, Illinois, and a private of Company "A," has kindly furnished us an account of the services of his regiment in the Mexican war, but as we have no official statement of the names or number of the Illinois men scattered through these regiments, we forbear to publish this as well as some other interesting matter which we have concerning the services of the regular regiments in the Mexican war.

In closing this memoranda of the services of the Illinois soldiers in the Black Hawk and Mexican wars, we can not forbear to mention that in the voluminous correspondence this office has had with the survivors of these wars, the idea seems to be universally prominent with them that the General Government should, in the exercise of that spirit of patriotic gratitude, heretofore manifested in favor of the soldiers of the revolution and of the war of 1812, grant equally to these survivors some further recognition of their services in the way of a pension. While it is no part of our duty, in editing this record, to attempt to support, or further any propositions asking such action by Congress, we may be allowed to say, without subjecting ourselves to criticism, that there is something in the appearance of the letters of these old veterans of a generation gone before, which appeals to our liveliest sympathies. They almost unanimously ask in their quavering and palsied penmanship, that the General Government make some additional provision to secure them against want in their old age.

BLACK HAWK WAR.

1832.

FIRST BRIGADE.

FIRST REGIMENT.

Capt. John Bays' Company

Of Illinois Mounted Volunteers, called into the service of the United States by the Governor of the State of Illinois, by his order of the 15th of May, 1832, from the date of its enrollment to the 12th day of August, 1832, when mustered out of service.

Name and Rank.	Residence.	Enrolled	Remarks.
Captain.		1832.	
John Bays	Gallatin Co.	June 16	Has two horses in service
First Lieutenant.			
William Robertson	"	"	Absent on furlough since August 9, 1832
Second Lieutenant.			
Daniel Wood	"	"	Absent on furlough since August 9, 1832
Sergeants.			
John Dawson	"	"	Detached from Co., on duty with main army.
Adran H. Davenport	"	"	Absent on furlough, by order of Brig.-Gen. [Atkinson
John T. Brown	"	"	
Solomon McCloud	"	"	Absent on furlough since August 9, 1832
Corporals.			
Isaiah W. Pettigrew	"	"	Absent on furlough since August 9, 1832
John Woods	"	"	Detached from Co., on duty with main army.
Thomas Smothers	"	"	Absent on furlough since August 9, 1832
Reuben Green	"	"	Detached from Co., on duty with main army.
Privates.			
Baker, Edmon	"	"	Absent on furlough since August 9, 1832
Bridges, James	"	"	
Bridges, Thomas L.	"	"	
Briant, John B.	"	"	Detached from Co., on duty with main army.
Brown, Daniel	"	"	On furlough since August 8, 1832
Brown, Samuel	"	"	Furloughed
Bays, David, Jr.	"	"	His horse lost, strayed or stolen
Cummons, William M	"	"	
Elder, John	"	"	Absent on furlough since August 9, 1832
Giles, Wm.	"	"	
Garner, Garrett	"	"	Detached on service with main army
Hargraves, Willis, Jr.	"	"	Detached from Co., on duty with main army.
Hargraves, Carter	"	"	
Henderson, Benj'min	"	"	
Hamons, Williams	"	"	
Hutson, John	"	"	Furloughed August 9, 1832
Johnson, William	"	"	Absent on surgeon's certif. since June 20, 1832
Kenrick, James	"	"	Absent on furl'h since July 16, '32; horse lost
Levil, Lewis	"	"	Absent on furlough
Mundine, Thomas S.	"	"	
McCaslin, James B.	"	"	His horse lost, strayed or stolen
Niswonger, Jefferson	"	"	Absent on furl'h since Aug. 9, '32; horse lost
Pruit, James	"	"	Furloughed Aug. 9, '32
Robinnett, John	"	"	Furloughed Aug. 4, '32; his horse lost
Reed, Green	"	"	Furloughed Aug. 4, '32

Name and Rank.	Residence.	Enrolled	Remarks.
Sands, John	Gallatin Co.	June 16	Absent on furlough since August 9, 1832
Thorn, Alexander	"	"	Detached from Co., on duty with main army.
Tadlock, Green	"	"	At Fort Hamilton, by order of Captain
Vaughn, Thomas	"	"	Absent on furlough since July 16, 1832
Williams, Ebenezer	"	"	" " " Aug. 9, 1832
Wrinkle, George	"	"	Furloughed; lost horse—b'ken down and left

I certify on honor that this muster roll exhibits the true state of the company under my command, and that the remarks set opposite the names of each officer and private are accurate and just.

(Signed.)   JOHN BAYS, CAPT.,
1st Reg't, 1st Brigade, Ill. Vol.

DIXON'S FERRY, Aug. 12, 1832.

Mustered out of service by me, by order of Maj.-Gen. W. Scott, commanding N. W. army.

(Signed.)   Z. C. PALMER, CAPT.,
6th U. S. Inf., Com. Post.

STATE OF ILLINOIS,
GALLATIN COUNTY,

This day personally appeared before me, the undersigned, Justice of the Peace in and for said county, Joseph E. Watkins, and made oath that he commanded a company of mounted volunteers in the service of the United States, in the year 1832, and that among his company who did actually arrive on the 10th day of June at Hennepin, on Illinois river, was George Wrinkle, who was a member of his said company regularly enrolled.
In testimony whereof I have set my hand and seal, this 5th June, 1834.

(Signed.)   T. D. HEWITT, J. P.

Personally appeared before me, the subscriber, a Justice of the Peace in Gallatin county, Lieut. Wm. Robinson, of Capt. Bays' company, and made oath that Lee Hargraves served as a private in Capt. Bays' company from the 16th of June to the 12th of August, 1832; also as a wagon-master, and is entitled to traveling pay up to Wilbourn, and from Fort Dixon to the place of his discharge, home.

(Signed.)   T. D. HEWITT, J. P.

EQUALITY, May 3, 1833.

CAPT. DAVID B. RUSSELL'S COMPANY

Of Mounted Volunteers of the State of Illinois, called into the service of the United States by the Governor of the State of Illinois, by his order of the 15th day of May, 1832, from the date of its enrollment to the 12th day of August, 1832, the time of its mustering out of service.

Name and Rank.	Residence.	Enrolled	Remarks.
Captain.		1832.	
David B. Russell	Gallatin Co.	June 16	Two horses in the service; lost one ax and spade in the water, $4.50.
First Lieutenant.			
William Pankey	"	"	
Sergeants.			
Geo. P. Keath	"	"	Absent on furlough
Claiborne Henders'n	"	"	
Thomas Pickering	"	"	
Stephen F. Mitchell	"	"	Detached from Co., on duty with main army.
Corporals.			
Jourdan Cook	"	"	Absent on furlough
Edward Hampton	"	"	Detached from Co., and on duty with main army; reported himself Aug. 12, 1832.
Robert Mitchell	"	"	
Thos. Dodds	"	"	Detached from Co., and on duty with main army; reported himself Aug. 12, 1832.
Bugleman.			
Jesse Hall	"	"	Absent on furlough
Privates.			
Abney, Matthew	"	"	Absent on furlough
Blackman, Josiah	"	"	
Cotner, Duncan	"	"	Absent on furlough

FIRST BRIGADE.

Name and Rank.	Residence.	Enrolled	Remarks.
		1832.	
Cook, Cullen.........	Gallatin Co..	June 16	Detached from Co., on duty with main army;
Covington, John.....	"	"	Absent on furlough ....[Reported Aug. 12
Duncan, Thomas....	"	"	Absent on furlough..... ....
Dunn, Squire........	"	"	
Fleming, Zachariah.	"	"	
Gaskins, William H.	"	"	Absent on furlough.............................
Gulley, Thomas	"	"	
Griffin, John........	"	"	" " granted on cert. of Surg.
Griffin, James S.....	"	"	" "
Hope, James.........	"	"	
Harris, Aulsey.......	"	"	
Harris, Gillam	"	"	Furlough granted on Surgeon's certificate...
Holland, James......	"	"	Absent on furlough.............................
Holmes, Jacob	"	"	" "
Hide, William........	"	"	" "
Howell, John........	"	"	" "
Howell, Riley........	"	"	
Hull, John..	"	"	
Hutchison, Wm. G..	"	"	
Ingram, Timothy....	"	"	
Johnson, John J.....	"	"	Absent on furlough; lost horse, bridle and
Pierson, Henry......	"	"	......................[saddle; value, $68.50
Russell, John	"	"	Absent on furlough.............................
Robinson, Mack.....	"	"	
Rood, Harvey........	"	"	Absent on furlough.............................
Rood, Ashby.	"	"	
Smothers, John	"	"	Detached from Co., on duty with main army;
Shoat, Levi	"	"	Absent on furlough .....[Reported Aug. 12,'32
Stiff, Lewis..........	"	"	
Stanley, Thomas.....	"	"	
Waggoner, John	"	"	Absent on furlough.............................

Muster roll of a detached part of Capt. Achilles Coffee's company, attached for the present to Capt. Russell's Company.

		1832.	
Sergeants.			
Samuel Karnes, 2d ..	Gallatin Co..	June 16	
John Gardner, 3d....	"	"	
William Chosier, 4th	"	"	
Privates.			
Abshear, Anderson..	"	"	
Carder, James.......	"	"	
Hanse, Peter	"	"	
Karnes, George.....	"	"	
Karnes, John........	"	"	
Karnes, James.......	"	"	
Martin, Jason	"	"	
Morris, Richmond...	"	"	
Medlin, Needum.....	"	"	
Pryor, Anderson	"	"	
Spruil, Pleasant.....	"	"	
Stricklin, William...	"	"	
Tong, Thomas	"	"	
Upchurch, John.....	"	"	
Upchurch, Thomas..	"	"	
Upchurch, Jonathan	"	"	

I certify on honor this muster roll exhibits the true state of the detachment under my command, and that the remarks set opposite the name of each officer and private, so far as made from my knowledge, are accurate and true, and so far as made from information I believe to be accurate.

                (Signed.)   DAVID B. RUSSELL, Capt.,
                                                1st Regt., 1st Brigade Ill. Vol.

Mustered out of service by me, by order of Major-Gen. Scott, commanding N. W. army.
                (Signed.)   Z. C. PALMER, Capt.,
                                                6th U. S. Inft., Com. Post.

Dixon's Ferry, Aug. 12, 1832.

Capt. Harrison Willson's Company

Of Illinois Mounted Volunteers, commanded by Lieut. John Willis, called into the service of the United States by the Governor of the State of Illinois, by his order of the 15th of May, 1832, from the date of its enrollment to the 12th day of August, 1832, when mustered out of service.

Name and Rank.	Residence.	Enrolled	Remarks.
Captain, Harrison Willson...	Gallatin Co...	1832. June 16	Detached from Co.; on duty with main army.
First Lieutenant. John Logston.........	"	"	Absent on Surgeon's certif., June 20, 1832....
Second Lieutenant. John Willis............	"	"	Sword lost with baggage wagon, or stolen..
Sergeants. Charles Hood.........	"	"	
Robert Sidle...........	"	"	Absent on furlough, Aug. 5, 1832.............
Solomon Brown.....	"	"	" " " Aug. 9, 1832...........
Mastin Alexander...	"	"	Lost 1 blanket, $1..............................
Corporals. Horatio Coffee......	"	"	Lost 1 saddle, valued at $14................
Isaac Crabtree........	"	"	Absent on furlough, Aug. 9, 1832............
William Keaton......	"	"	Lost 1 bridle and 1 quilt, $4.................
Richard Tarlton......	"	"	
Privates. Alexander, Rheubin.	"	"	Lost 1 blanket................................
Barger, Richard A. S.	"	"	
Burnet, Hiram........	"	"	Absent on furlough, 9th Aug., 1832..........
Baker, James..........	"	"	
Clack, John T.........	"	"	Lost 1 mare, saddle, blankets, saddle-bags..
Cox, William..........	"	"	
Coop, William........	"	"	Detailed from Co.; on duty with main army.
Caldwell, John........	"	"	" " " " " "
Davis, James M......	"	"	
Davis, Francis.........	"	"	
Ellis, William.........	"	"	Absent on furlough...........................
Giberson, William...	"	"	Detailed on furlough.
Hogan, Richard......	"	"	
Holey, Henry.........	"	"	Absent on furlough, Aug. 9, 1832. Lost a horse
Huston, Even.........	"	"	Absent, and on duty with main army.........
Jones, Fountain W...	"	"	
Jacobs, Page...........	"	"	Absent on furlough, Aug. 9, 1832.............
Kirkendal, Robert...	"	"	Lost 2 blankets...............................
Logston, Joseph......	"	"	Absent on furlough, Aug. 9, 1832.............
Pool, Orvel.............	"	"	
Peeples, James C.....	"	"	
Scrogins, Barton.....	"	"	
Taylor, Washington.	"	"	
Willis, Jacob...........	"	"	
Woodle, Andrew.....	"	"	

STATE OF ILLINOIS, }
GALLATIN COUNTY. } set:

This 6th day of May, 1833, Captain Harrison Willson personally appeared before the undersigned, an acting Justice of the Peace in and for said county, and made oath that Mr. Alexander H. Hall, was enrolled in his (Willson's) company, as a volunteer in Gallatin county; that at Fort Wilbourn he was mustered into the service of the United States, in the war against the Sac Indians, on the 16th of June, 1832, in said company; that he, said Hall, was on the day after transferred to Gen. Posey's staff, as volunteer aid, and in a few days thereafter furloughed to return home, as he is informed.

(Signed) H. WILLSON, CAPT

Subscribed and sworn before me this 6th day of May, 1833.
(Signed) JAMES CALDWELL, J. P.

I certify on honor, that Wm. M. Wallace, Jno. McClernand and Mershall Rawlands volunteered as privates in Capt. Willson's company Ill. Militia and belonged to said company when it was organized at Fort Wilbourn. They afterwards were appointed on the staff and commissioned by the Governor, viz: Wallace as Brigade Paymaster, McClernand and Rawlins as Assistant Brigade Quartermasters. They served during the campaign and were mustered out at Fort Dixon, the 14th of August, 1832; they are at least entitled to private's pay.

(Signed.) A. POSEY,
EQUALITY, May 4th, 1833. late Brig.-Gen.

Capt. Joel Holliday's Company

1st Regiment, 1st Brigade of Illinois Mounted Volunteers, called into the service of the United States, on the requisition of Gen. Atkinson, by the Governor's proclamation, dated 15th May, 1832. Mustered out, Aug. 16, 1832.

Name and Rank.	Residence.	Enrolled	Remarks.
Captains.		1832	
James Caldwell	Gallatin Co	....	Resigned about the 19th of June
Joel Holliday	"	June 16	
First Lieutenant.			
Turner Cook	"	"	Absent on furlough, Aug. 5, 1832
Second Lieutenant.			
John J. Dean	"	"	Lost 1 pistol, wallet and saddle-bags
Sergeants.			
Benjamin Kinsall	"	"	
Robert R Deull	"	"	
Quinzey Right	"	"	
Thos. V. Swearenger	"	"	
Corporals.			
David Kinsall	"	"	......[tered out of service.
John Newman	"	"	Detached under Capt. Bays; supposed mus-
E. B. Puckett	"	"	Absent on furlough, July 1, 1832
Boni Hubbs	"	"	Detached under Capt. Bays; supposed mus-[tered out of service.
Privates.			
Adams, John	"	"	Absent; I know not whether with or without
Bish, George	"	"	Absent on detached service............[leave.
Barker, William	"	"	" "
Barker, Jesse	"	"	
Brown, Adonijah	"	"	
Bozarth, David	"	"	
Cusack, James	"	"	Absent; I know not whether with or without
Hays, Solomon	"	"	..........[leave.
Haskins, Jas. R	"	"	
Herod, Jno. W	"	"	Absent on furlough
Jones, Jonathan	"	"	
Luther, Ezra G	"	"	Lost 1 pair saddle-bags and wallet
Nelson, Stephen	"	"	
Powell, Thomas	"	"	Lost 1 horse on forced march
Quigley, Aaron	"	"	
Stiff, Richard	"	"	
Trousdale, James	"	"	
Thompson, Matthew	"	"	
Venson, Charles	"	"	

The following are supposed to be mustered out of service under Capt. Bays:

Name and Rank.	Residence.	Enrolled	Remarks.
Privates.		1832	
Brown, James	Gallatin Co	June 16	Detached under Capt. Bays
Burris, Thomas	"	"	" " "
Crissop, James	"	"	" " "
Clayton, William	"	"	" " "
Dunson, John	"	"	" " "
Fouch, Levi	"	"	" " "
Fouch, John	"	"	" " "
Heraldson, William	"	"	" " "
Hutchcraft, Elijah	"	"	" " "
Johnson, Jas. B	"	"	" " "
Morrow, Thomas	"	"	" " "
Morrow, Forquer	"	"	" " "
Patillo, Alexander	"	"	" " "
Ralls, Nathaniel	"	"	" " "
Sherwood, Hugh B	"	"	" " "
Sherwood, Thomas	"	"	" " "
Shoemaker, William	"	"	" " "
Smith, Peter	"	"	" " "
Sampson, William	"	"	" " "
Westbrook, Samuel	"	"	" " "
Williams, James	"	"	" " "
Williams, Henry B	"	"	" " "
Wood, Mason	"	"	" " "

Name and Rank.	Residence.	Enrolled	Remarks.
Dake, Arnold B			Refused to march with company to Koskana.
Edwards, Phillip			" " " "
Hughston, Jonathan			" " " "
Keeny, Jonathan			" " " "
Lafferty, William			" " " "
Reynolds, Jas. L			" " " "
Tally, Amos			" " " "

This company was enrolled by Capt. Jas. Caldwell, who commanded it until it entered the service of the United States, when he quit his command, and, in some three or four days after, the present Captain was elected. This company, individually at their own expense, furnished six days' rations for themselves when they marched from home to enter the service of the United States. They have each received but one-half bushel of corn as forage during the whole campaign, and the officers have drawn but one ration in kind per day. This company was mustered, and an election of officers had, on the 12th of May, 1832, marched for Fort Wilbourn June 1st, and was received into service June 16, 1832.

CAPT. ARCHILAUS COFFEY'S COMPANY

Of the 1st Regiment, 1st Brigade Illinois Volunteers, called into the service of the United States, on the requisition of Gen. Atkinson, by the Governor's proclamation dated May 15, 1832. Mustered out, August 12, 1832.

Name and Rank.	Residence.	Enrolled	Remarks.
Captain.		1832	
Archilaus Coffey	Gallatin Co.	June 16	Furloughed at battle ground August 3
First Lieutenant.			
Daniel Botright	"	"	Furl. on Surgeon's certificate July 15, 1832
Second Lieutenant.			
Willis Stricklen	"	"	Furl. by Gen. Atkinson, from Prairie du Chien
Corporals.			
Wiley Roberts	"	"	Furloughed to return home, Aug. 9, 1832
John Rhyon	"	"	
David A. Grable	"	"	" attend sick, July 15, 1832
Privates.			
Abner, Henry	"	"	Furl. on Surgeon's certificate July 15, 1832
Barger, Isaac	"	"	Furloughed to return home Aug. 9, 1832
Bond, George	"	"	" " " " "
Bond, Stephen	"	"	" " " " "
Coy, John	"	"	" " " " "
Hall, Jonathan	"	"	
Hawkins, James	"	"	Furl. on Surgeon's certificate July 15, 1832
Hedge, James	"	"	Furloughed to return home Aug. 9, 1832
Isom, Richard	"	"	Furl. on Surgeon's certificate July 3, 1832
Lewis, Abraham	"	"	Furloughed to return home Aug. 9, 1832
Oldham, Thomas	"	"	Furl. Aug. 3; lost horse, saddle and bridle
Pogue, James	"	"	
Richey, John P	"	"	Furloughed to return home Aug. 9, 1832
Ryon, William	"	"	" " " " "
Smith, John	"	"	" " " " "
Smith, John H	"	"	" " " " "
Whitesides, Thomas	"	"	
Ware, Robert	"	"	Furl. on Surgeon's certificate July 15, 1832

Mustered out of service by Capt. Palmer:

Sergeants.		1832.	[Ferry, Aug. 12, 1832.
Samuel Ravney, 2d	Gallatin Co.	June 16	Mus. out under Capt. D. B. Russell, at Dixon's
John Garner, 3d	"	"	
Wm. Chosier, 4th	"	"	
Privates.			
Alshear, Anderson	"	"	
Carder, James K	"	"	
Hause, Peter	"	"	

FIRST BRIGADE.

Name and Rank.	Residence.	Enrolled	Remarks.
		1832.	
Karns, James	Gallatin Co.	June 16.	
Karns, John	"	"	
Karns, George	"	"	
Martin, Jason	"	"	
Medling, Nodum	"	"	
Morris, Richmond	"	"	
Prior, Anderson	"	"	
Strickland, William	"	"	
Spruel, Pleasant	"	"	Mus. out under Capt. D. B. Russell, at Dixon's
Tongue, Thomas	"	"	..........[Ferry, Aug. 12, 1832.
Upchurch, John	"	"	
Upchurch, Jonathan	"	"	
Upchurch, Thomas	"	"	

Supposed to have been mustered out with Col. Ewing's Regt., by Capt. Palmer:

		1832.	
Corporal.			
Gasaway, Hamilton	Gallatin Co.	June 16	
Private.			
Carney, David	"	"	

Discharged:

		1832	
First Sergeant.			
Aden Warner	Gallatin Co.	June 16	Discharged by Lieut. R. Anderson, A. I. Gen., [Aug. 16, 1832, by reason expiration service.
Privates.			
Cox, John	"	"	Dis. on Surg. certif. of disability, by Gen. At-
Fletcher, Wesley	"	"	..........[kinson, June 18, 1832.
Garret, William	"	"	Dis. by Lieut. R. Anderson, A. I. Gen., Aug.
Strickland, Henry	"	"	..........[16, 1832; expiration service.

I certify on honor, that I have carefully examined this muster roll, and that I have this 25th day of Sept., 1832, signed this roll,—the Captain having called on me to certify as above, to the state of his company, and to account for the absence of the company from the place designated for being mustered out of the service of the United States. The company to be considered as having been mustered out on the same day its Regt. was mustered out.

    (Signed.)   ROBERT ANDERSON,
                Lieut. and Ass't. Insp. Gen.

I certify that it was impossible for me to reach the place of mustering out, in consequence of the loss of my horse.
    (Signed.)   ARCHILAUS COFFEY, Capt.

Transportation furnished by the United States, from Galena to St. Louis, for all of the company who were furloughed after the battle of the 2d of August, 1832. This company was organized May 12th, 1832. Marched for the frontier May 26th, 1832. Mustered into the service of the United States June 16, 1832. Mustered out, Aug. 12, 1832.

SECOND REGIMENT.

Capt. George P. Bowyer's Company.

Of Mounted Volunteers of the State of Illinois, called into the service of the United States by the Governor of the State, by his order of the 15th day of May, 1832, from the date of its enrollment to the 7th day of August, 1832, the time of mustering out of service. Enrolled for 90 days.

Name and Rank.	Residence.	Enrolled	Remarks.
Captain.		1832.	
George P. Bowyer...	Franklin Co..	June 16	Had two horses in service....................
First Lieutenant.			
Jacob Philips........	" "	" "	....
Second Lieutenant.			
Thomas P. Moore ...	" "	" "	Lost clothing, etc., valued at $9.50 ....
Sergeants.			
Thomas Adams, 1st..	" "	" "	Absent on furlough ....
Jacob Chark, 2d	" "	" "	" "
Edward Franklin, 3d	" "	" "	Left at Fort Hamilton, sick ....
Corporals.			
William Fleming, 1st	" "	" "	Bridle and tomah'wk lost, swim'g Pecatonica
William Akins, 2d ..	" "	" "	Coffee pot lost; value 62½ cents................
Augustus Adams, 4th	" "	" "	Absent on furlough ....
Bugler.			
William Whittington	" "	" "	Absent on furlough ....
Privates.			
Adams, Benjamin ...	" "	" "	....
Bevers, Thomas	" "	" "	....
Bowling, James	" "	" "	....
Bowling, Benjamin..	" "	" "	Coffee and saddle-blanket lost; value $4.50...
Bowyer, Henry......	" "	" "	Bridle lost; value $2.00.........................
Berry, John	" "	" "	Absent on furlough ....
Bailey, Jacob........	" "	" "	....
Browning, James ...	" "	" "	Transferred to Capt. West's company ....
Clampet, William....	" "	" "	....
Cleveland, Evan.....	" "	" "	Saddle-blanket lost; value $2.50................
Clark, John	" "	" "	Absent on furlough ....
Cleveland, Jesse	" "	" "	....
Clark, Reuben	" "	" "	....
Due, John P.........	" "	" "	Absent on furlough ....
Dement, John	Fayette Co..	" "	Promoted to Major of Spy Bat., 1st Brig......
Dillingham, Vachel..	Franklin Co..	" "	....
Estes, Absalom......	" "	" "	....
Farris, James........	" "	" "	....
Gifford, Joseph......	" "	" "	Absent on furlough ....
Hail, Thomas........	" "	" "	Cloak and sack lost; value $7.00................
Jourdan, Moses	" "	" "	Promoted Sergt.-Major; absent on furlough.
Jourden, Elijah......	" "	" "	....
Jourden, James	" "	" "	Absent on furlough ....
Morgan, Nathaniel..	" "	" "	....
Neal, Aaron..........	" "	" "	Transferred from Stephenson's Co.; on furl,.
Plaisters, James	" "	" "	Absent on furlough ....
Redburn, Abraham..	" "	" "	....
Robertson, Garrett..	" "	" "	Absent on furlough ....
Richardson, A. W...	" "	" "	....
Scribner, John	" "	" "	Frying-pan and tin bucket lost; value $1.00 ..
Summers, James.....	" "	" "	Sent to Fort Hamilton on duty; care of sick.
Summers, Noah	" "	" "	" " sick
Schoolcraft, James..	" "	" "	" " on duty; care of sick.
Slater, John.........	" "	" "	....

FIRST BRIGADE.   11

Name and Rank.	Residence.	Enrolled	Remarks.
Whittington, Benj...	Franklin Co...	June 16	Tin bucket lost; value 37½ cents ....
Whittington, James.	"	"	Absent on furlough ....
Williams, Benjamin.	"	"	
Ward, William	"	"	Blanket lost, valued at $2.50 ....
Western, Joseph	"	"	Transferred to Capt. Drennan's company ....

I certify on honor that this muster roll exhibits the true state of the detachment under my command, and that the remarks set opposite the name of each officer and private are accurate and just.
      (Signed.)   GEO. P. BOWYER, CAPT.,
               2d Regt., 1st Brig. Ill. Vol.

              DIXON FERRY, August 7, 1832.
Mustered out of service by me, by order of Maj.-Gen. Scott, commanding N. W. Army.
      (Signed.)   Z. C. PALMER, CAPT.,
              6th U. S. Inft. Com. Post.

STATE OF ILLINOIS, } ss.
FRANKLIN COUNTY. }

I, George P. Bowyer, do solemnly swear that Jno. Slater and Alexander W. Richardson were regularly enrolled in the service of the United States in my company, at Fort Wilbourn, on June 16, 1832, and that they served the full period of time for which they were enrolled, and were regularly discharged at Fort Dixon, by Capt. Palmer, on a detached roll; and that they are justly entitled to full pay and allowance for said service (and, as I am informed, said detached roll was lost or mislaid).
      (Signed.)   GEO. P. BOWYER, CAPT.
Subscribed and sworn to this 9th May, 1833.
      (Signed.)   JOHN Y. DAVIS, J. P.

CAPT. WM. J. STEPHENSON'S COMPANY

Of Mounted Volunteers, called into the service of the United States by the Governor of the State of Illinois, by his order of the 15th day of May, 1832, from its enrollment to the 7th day of August, 1832, when mustered out of service. Enrolled for 90 days.

Name and Rank.	Residence.	Enrolled	Remarks.
Captain.		1832.	
Wm. J. Stephenson	Franklin Co...	June 16.	Gray mare lost in service; appraised at $65...
Second Lieutenant.			
Tramel Ewing.......	"	"	Absent on furlough ....
Sergeants.			
John P. Maddox.....	"	"	Absent on furlough ....
Anderson P. Corder.	"	"	Lost blanket in battle; appraised at $2 ......
Henry Hays..........	"	"	Lost horse and equipage; appraised $66.37½.
John T. Knox........	"	"	On duty at Apple River Fort.................
Corporals.			
Thos. Provence, 1st.	"	"	
Michael Rawlins, 2d.	"	"	
Musician.			
Walter B. Scates	"	"	Lost blanket, etc., in battle; appraised at $6..
Privates.			
Bobbitt, John........	"	"	Absent on furlough ....
Denning, Josiah B..	"	"	
Eubanks, Elisha.....	"	"	Discharged at Ft. Wilbourn; to rec. full pay.
Farris, Anderson P..	"	"	Lost horse, arms, blanket; appraised $84.50..
Garrett, Hezekiah ..	"	"	Absent on furlough ....
Garrett, Robert......	"	"	" "
Gassaway, William..	"	"	
Hickman, Benj. F...	"	"	Appointed Governor's Aid, June 17, 1832 ......
Hays, John	"	"	Lost bridle in battle; appraised at $1.50 ....
Hubbard, Wm. A....	"	"	
Hillen, Lewis	"	"	Lost blanket in battle; appraised $2.50.........
Jones, Nathaniel	"	"	
Knox, Thomas.......	"	"	
Lynch, Larkin.......	"	"	
Maddox, Wm. P.....	"	"	Lost horse and equipage; appraised at $36.35.

Name and Rank.	Residence.	Enrolled	Remarks.
Miller, Andrew	Franklin Co..	June 16.	Blanket in battle; appraised at $2.50
Neal, Moses	"	"	Appointed Quartermaster Sergt. 2d Regt., 1st
Pope, Benj. W	"	"	Absent on furlough....[Brig. Ill. Mounted Vol.
Rotramel, Henry	"	"	
Robertson, Andrew	"	"	
Rawlings, Ezekiel	"	"	On duty at Apple River Fort
Rea, Wilson	"	"	Discharged at Ft. Wilbourn; to rec. full pay.
Swafford, Harvey	"	"	Blanket in battle; appraised at $2.50
Silkwood, H. M	"	"	Absent on furlough
Talbot, Benjamin	"	"	Absent on furl., or discharged at Ft. Wilbourn

I certify on honor that this muster roll exhibits the true state of the company under my command, and that the remarks set opposite the name of each officer and soldier are accurate and just.

(Signed.)   WM. J. STEPHENSON, CAPT.,
of the 2d Regt., 1st Brig.

DIXON'S FERRY, Aug. 7, 1832.
Mustered out of service by me by order of Maj.-Gen. Scott, commanding N. W. army.
(Signed.)   Z. C. PALMER, CAPT.,
6th U. S. Inft., Com. Post.

CAPT. OBEDIAH WEST'S COMPANY

Of Mounted Volunteers, called into the service of the United States by the Governor of Illinois, by his order of the 15th of May, 1832, from the date of its enrollment to the 6th day of August, 1832, when mustered out of service. (Company now under command of 1st Lieut. Robt. West, commanding.) Enrolled for 90 days.

Name and Rank.	Residence.	Enrolled	Remarks.
Captain.		1832.	
Obediah West	Franklin Co..	June 16	Absent on furlough
First Lieutenant.			
Robert West	"	"	
Second Lieutenant.			
Hugh Parks	"	"	Absent on furlough
Sergeants.			
Wilie Scott, 1st	"	"	Horse lost in service
William Henry, 4th	"	"	Absent on furlough
Corporal.			
Moses Odum, 3d	"	"	
Privates.			
Browning, James	"	"	
Bradley, Pleasant	"	"	Absent on furlough
Beasley, Washington	"	"	"
Franklin, Edward	"	"	
Groves, Isaac	"	"	
Hooker, Jabez	"	"	Absent on furlough
Henry, Augustus	"	"	"
Joiner, Jiles	"	"	" " horse lost in service
Layman, Henry	"	"	
Meredith, Junior	"	"	
Murphy, William	"	"	
Provence, Albert	"	"	
Pulley, Thomas	"	"	Absent on furlough
Parks, Samuel	"	"	
Price, Richard	Pike Co	"	Absent on furlough
Parks, Andrew	Franklin Co..	"	Tent cloth (private property) lost, value, $3
Rich, William	"	"	
Ran, William	"	"	
Roper, Seth	"	"	
Springs, David H	"	"	
Worthen, Robert	"	"	
Ward, John	"	"	Absent on furlough
Ward, Dickson	"	"	"
Watson, Robert	"	"	
Youngblood, Isaac	"	"	
Zacharias, George	"	"	

FIRST BRIGADE. 13

STATE OF ILLINOIS, } ss:
FRANKLIN COUNTY,

We, John Ewing, Col. of the 2d Regt., and Obediah West, Captain in said Regiment, do solemnly swear that John Cunningham was enrolled in Capt. West's company, at Fort Wilbourn, on the 16th of June, 1832, in the service of the United States, served up to 12th of August faithfully, but on account of being absent on detached service, was not mustered out of service with his proper company. We further state on oath that it is our opinion that said John is fully entitled to pay and all allowances for said service.

(Signed.) JOHN EWING, COL.
(Signed.) OBEDIAH WEST, CAPT.

Subscribed and sworn before me the 9th of May, 1833.
(Signed.) JOHN T. DAVIS, J. P.

CAPT. CHARLES DUNN'S COMPANY

Of Mounted Volunteers, called into the service of the United States by the Governor of Illinois, by his order of May 15, 1832, from the date of its enrollment to August 13, 1832, the time of mustering out of service.

Name and Rank.	Residence.	Enrolled	Remarks.
Captain,		1832	
Charles Dunn.........	Pope Co......	June 16	Two horses in service..........................
First Lieutenant.			
Joseph Neal............	"	"	Left at Fort Hamilton, sick................
Second Lieutenants.			
John Raum............	"	"	Promoted to Brig. Maj., June 16, '32, 1st Brig.
James H. McColugh..	"	"	Elected and commis'd in place John Raum, [promoted June 16, 1832.
Sergeants.			
Jesse R. Pratt.........	"	"	Absent on furlough dated July 31, 1832 . .....
Andrew H. Drinnon..	"	"	Appointed 1st Sergt., in place of Pratt, July [31, 1832; horse lost, strayed or stolen.
Corporals.			
James F. Johnston..	"	"	Prom. Reg. Q. M. July 1, '32; mus. out as such
John Hamilton.......	"	"	U. S. halter lost..................................
Jason B. Smith.......	"	"	Absent on furlough...............................
Privates.			
Arnold, James.......	"	"	U. S. camp-ax lost...............................
Anderson, William..	"	"	
Bruce, David........	"	"	
Bruce, Thomas......	"	"	
Barr, William A.....	"	"	
Cowsert, Geo. W....	"	"	Absent on furlough..............................
Dobbins, John M....	"	"	Left sick at Fort Hamilton.....................
Hawley, Joshua S...	"	"	U. S. halter lost..................................
Hughes, Richard....	"	"	
Harper, Joseph......	"	"	U. S. halter lost..................................
Hall, Thomas........	"	"	U. S. tin bucket and camp-ax lost............
Hodge, John P......	"	"	
Kennedy, Jacob.....	"	"	U. S. halter lost..................................
McCool, John........	"	"	
Merow, John........	"	"	
Paisily, William M..	"	"	
Pearce, Daniel......	"	"	Deserted July 20, 1832.........................
Palmore, Willie R..	"	"	
Palmore, Calvin H..	"	"	U. S. hatchet lost...............................
Puttello, Nathan....	"	"	Absent on furlough.............................
Pratt, Mathew Y....	"	"	
Paisley, John........	"	"	U. S. camp-ax, halter, bayonet-scabbard lost
Rose, James	"	"	
Slankard, Harrison..	"	"	Horse lost, strayed or stolen.................
Smith, Hiram G.....	"	"	Absent on furlough.............................
Wiley, Joseph.......	"	"	Left sick at Fort Hamilton....................
Whiteside, John.....	"	"	Absent on furlough dated July 31, 1832.........

Capt. Jonathan Durman's Company

Of Mounted Volunteers of Illinois, called into the service of the United States by the Governor of the State of Illinois, by his order of May 15, 1832, from the date of its enrollment to Aug. 12, 1832, the time of its mustering out of service.

Name and Rank.	Residence.	Enrolled	Remarks.
Captain. Jonathan Durman	Pope Co	1832 June 16	Two horses and one servant in service
First Lieutenant. Simon S. Bargar	"	"	
Second Lieutenant. Jacob Benyard	"	"	
Sergeants.			
John B. Witt	"	"	
Thomas M. Ellis	"	"	
Green B. Veatch	"	"	
Alfred M. Hazel	"	"	
Corporals.			
John Lewis	"	"	
Thomas Matthews	"	"	
Privates.			
Anderson, Andrew	"	"	Left sick at Fort Wilbourn
Allen, Marshall	"	"	Horse lost in service
Banty, Jesse	"	"	
Baily, James	"	"	
Bowman, David	"	"	Absent on furlough
Crawford, James	"	"	
Carlyle, William	"	"	Absent on furlough
Cowsent, Samuel	"	"	Ord. to Ft. Hamilton on duty; horse lost, shot
Davis, Colman	"	"	
Demick, Judetham C	"	"	
Dorset, William	"	"	
Holland, James	"	"	
Hobbs, Ezekial	"	"	Deserted July 20, 1832
Harlice, William	"	"	Left on duty at Ft. Wilbourn to attend sick
Hobbs, Christopher	"	"	Absent on furlough, granted on Surg's certif.
Jones, Alfred	"	"	"
King, Anderson	"	"	
King, John	"	"	
Lewis, Joseph L	"	"	Absent on furlough
Lauderdale, John	"	"	
Martin, Isaac L	"	"	
Noaks, Abraham	"	"	Left sick at Fort Hamilton
Perrin, James	"	"	
Raney, Robert R	"	"	Absent on furlough; horse lost in service
Slankard, Jacob	"	"	
Williams, John	"	"	Left at Fort Funk sick
Williams, James	"	"	"
Williams, Josiah	"	"	" to attend the sick
Williams, Isom	"	"	
Watkins, Isaac F	"	"	Left at Funk's Fort to attend the sick
Wallace, Squire	"	"	" sick
West, Joseph	Franklin Co	"	Det. by cons'nt from Capt. West's Co.; att'ch'd to Capt. Durman's.

Capt. Holman's Company

Of Illinois Mounted Volunteers, called into the service of the United States by the Governor of the State, by his order of May 15, 1832, from the date of its enrollment to the 2d day of August, 1832, when mustered out of service.

Name and Rank.	Residence.	Enrolled	Remarks.
Captain. Armstead Holman		1832 June 15	
First Lieutenant. James Duncan		"	

FIRST BRIGADE.

Name and Rank.	Residence.	Enrolled	Remarks.
Second Lieutenant.		1832.	
Squire Howell		June 15	
Sergeants.			
O. H. Willey		"	
Joel Norris		"	
Abraham Duncan		"	One blanket lost in service
Wintfroy L. Crain		"	
Corporals.			
Manuel Hunter		"	
John Spiller		"	One horse lost in service
Willis Tiner		"	
James Norris		"	
Musician.			
Thomas C. Lowden		"	
Privates.			
Boid, Larry		"	
Crain, Noah		"	
Crain, Spencer		"	
Crain, Wm. B		"	
Crain, Manuel R		"	
Crain, Champ T		"	
Chittey, Alfred		"	
Daniel, Thomas		"	
Durock, Lewis		"	
Duncan, Wm. H		"	
Fisher, Thomas		"	
Fisher, Solomon		"	
Gulley, Isaac		"	One U. S. scabbard belt lost
Hail, Thos		"	" " and one horse
Hunter, George W		"	
Herring, Reuben		"	One horse lost in service
Hancock, Thomas		"	
Hindman, Wm		"	
Huffman, Westley		"	
James, Thomas		"	
Lastly, John		"	
Lewis, Isaac		"	
McAlley, Archibald		"	
Moake, Ezekiel		"	
Nelson, Morgan		"	
Nelson, James M		"	Furloughed (inability for service) June 20, '32.
Phenix, John		"	
Russell, James S		"	
Rowland, Wm		"	
Russell, Phillip J		"	
Rawls, Wm		"	
Rawls, Harris		"	
Ryburn, Byrd T		"	
Spiller, John B		"	
Stroud, Daniel		"	
Stroud, Levi		"	
Spiller, Martin B		"	
Stack, John		"	
Tarpley, Wm. H		"	
Tippey, James		"	
Tiner, Isham		"	One belt and tomahawk lost in service
Tiner, Joshua		"	
Williams, Tippo S		"	
Williams, David		"	
Yancey, Hiram		"	
Yancey, Wm. R		"	

THIRD REGIMENT.

Capt. Ardin Biggerstaff's Company

Of Mounted Volunteers of Illinois, called into the service of the United States by the Governor of Illinois, by his order of May 15, 1832, from the date of its enrollment to the 13th day of August, 1832, the time of mustering out of service. Enrolled for 90 days.

Name and Rank.	Residence.	Enrolled	Remarks.
Captain. Ardin Biggerstaff	Hamilton Co.	1832. June 16	
First Lieutenant. Lewis Lane	"	"	
Second Lieutenant. Wesley W. Wiltes	"	"	On furlough
Sergeants.			
Wesley W. Gholston	"	"	On furlough
James M. Wilson	"	"	
James Allen, Sr.	"	"	One saddle lost; value $10
William Fuller	"	"	
Corporals.			
Joshua G. Weaver	"	"	One tent cloth lost on forc'd m'rch, val. $4.68¾
Benjamin I. Allen	"	"	
Grandville Gholston	"	"	
Solomon Skelton	"	"	Appointed 4th Corporal
Fifer. Elisha Everett	"	"	
Trumpeter. Adonijah G. Grimes	"	"	On furlough
Privates.			
Allen, John	"	"	
Allen, James, Jr	"	"	
Bryant, James H.	"	"	
Bryant, William	"	"	
Blake, James	"	"	On furlough
Cronch, Adam	"	"	
Cook, Ellison	"	"	
Campbell, William	"	"	
Drew, William	"	"	Tent-cloth lost, escap'g from Ind's; also coat.
Everett, Elijah	"	"	
Gallaher, James F.	"	"	Lost one bayonet belt; supposed stolen
Gibson, John	"	"	
Hynes, Andrew S.	"	"	
Johnson, Saml.	"	"	On furlough
Jourdan, Jesse	"	"	
Jenkins, Thos, S.	"	"	
Johnson, William	"	"	On furlough
Lowry, John	"	"	
Mayberry, David R.	"	"	On furlough
Mayberry, Frederick	"	"	Discharged June 20, 1832, as sick
Morris, Daniel	"	"	Lost one bayonet and bayonet belt
Martin, Saml	"	"	On furlough
Moore, Jesse	"	"	
Porter, Elbridge G.	"	"	"
Riley, William	"	"	
Riley, F. A.	"	"	
Richey, J. M.	"	"	On furlough; lost horse in action, value, $100
Sexton, Charles	"	"	On furlough
Stull, Nicholas	"	"	
Steerman, N. D.	"	"	

FIRST BRIGADE.

Name and Rank.	Residence.	Enrolled	Remarks.
Steerman, W. M.	Hamilton Co.	June 16	
Shelton, Joseph	"	"	Promoted to Major June 16, 1832; lost horse
Trotter, Archibald	"	"	
Trammel, Nicholas	"	"	
Thomason, Jos. F.	"	"	
Wheeler, Washingt'n	"	"	On furlough
Wheeler, John	"	"	

I certify on honor that this muster roll exhibits the state of the company under my command, and that the "remarks" set opposite the name of each officer and soldier are, to the best of my knowledge, accurate and just.

(Signed.)   ARDIN BIGGERSTAFF, Capt.,
Com. 2d Co., 2d Bat. 3d Regt., 1st Brig., Ill. Mounted Vol.

Station—Dixon Ferry.   Date—Aug. 13, 1832.

Capt. John Onslott's Company

Of the 3d Regiment of the 1st Brigade of Illinois Mounted Volunteers, called into the service of the United States, on the requisition of Gen. Atkinson, by the Governor's proclamation, dated ——, 1832; mustered out August 15, 1832, by order of Brig.-Gen. Atkinson.

Name and Rank.	Residence.	Enrolled	Remarks.
Captain.		1832.	
John Onslott	Clay Co.	June 16.	Elected Captain May 29, 1832
First Lieutenant.			
Trussey P. Hanson	"	"	Elected First Lieutenant May 29, 1832
Second Lieutenant.			
Alfred J. Moore	"	"	Elected Second Lieutenant May 29, 1832
Sergeants.			
Cyrus Wright	"	"	Appointed May 29, 1832
Elisha Bashford	"	"	
Arch. T. Patterson	"	"	" " [May 29, 1832
James Tompkins	"	"	Supposed disch'g'd by Gen. Scott; appointed
Corporals.			
Samuel Whiteley	"	"	Appointed May 29, 1832
Strother B. Walker	"	"	
Joseph Whiteley	"	"	" "
Francis Herman	"	"	
Privates.			
Ano, James T.	"	"	
Creek, Jefferson	"	"	
Cook, James	"	"	On furlough, by order of Col. Leech
Carbaugh, Sol. B.	"	"	" " "
Chamberlin, Young.	"	"	
Campbell, Augur	"	"	
Daniels, Levi	"	"	
Fitzgerald, A. S.	"	"	Broke down in service; furloughed Aug. 9, '32
Lethcoe, Joseph	"	"	
Logan, Russell	"	"	On furlough by order of Major Campbell
McDaniel, Hugh	"	"	Supposed discharged by Gen. Scott
McDaniel, Robert	"	"	
McGrew, John	"	"	On furlough, Aug. 9, 1832
McKenney, James	"	"	Broke down in service; furl. by Maj. Campbell
Moseley, Bennett W.	"	"	
Mortin, Perkey	"	"	Supposed discharged by Gen. Scott
Nicholson, John G.	"	"	
Nelson, James	"	"	On furlough by order of Col. Leech
Rogers, Isaac	"	"	
Rogers, Thomas	"	"	
Skief, Jesse	"	"	
Songer, Abram	"	"	
Stallings, Lockhard.	"	"	
Sincoe, David	"	"	On furlough by order of Major Campbell
Sutton, John	"	"	On furlough, Aug. 1, 1832
Speaker, John	"	"	On furlough, Aug. 9, 1832

Name and Rank.	Residence.	Enrolled	Remarks.
		1832.	
Tarter, Frederick	Clay Co	June 16.	
Van Cleave, James	"	"	
Walker, Isaac	"	"	On furlough, Aug. 9, 1832.
Wickersham, Jas. L.	"	"	On furlough, Aug. 1, 1832.
Whiteley, Martin	"	"	

Took up line of March from Clay county June 2, 1832. Mustered into U. S. service June 16, 1832. Captain and other officers have drawn but one ration in kind each day, and but one-half bushel of corn for horse during the campaign, and eight days' rations to travel home on.

(Signed.)

On this 12th day of August, 1832.

JOHN ONSLOTT, Capt.

Capt. James Hall's Company

Of Mounted Volunteers of Illinois, called into the service of the United States by the Governor of Illinois, by his order of May 15, 1832, from the date of its enrollment to August 13, 1832, the time of mustering out of service.

Name and Rank.	Residence.	Enrolled	Remarks.
Captain.		1832.	
James Hall	Hamilton Co.	June 16	One iron-gray horse lost; value, $100.
First Lieutenant.			
John Burton	"	"	Absent on furlough.
Second Lieutenant.			
John Townsand	"	"	Absent on furlough.
Sergeants.			
Milton Carpenter	"	"	Absent on furlough.
Robert Witt	"	"	" " One mare stolen; value, $100
John M. Smith	"	"	
Alfred More	"	"	
Corporals.			
John Heard	"	"	Discharged ——, 1832, by Capt. Palmer.
Charles Heard	"	"	[valued at $80
Keling T. Maulding	"	"	Absent on furlough. One bay horse stolen,
Willis Atkinson	"	"	
Bugleman.			
Clinton Hopkins	"	"	
Privates.			
Adair, Phillip	"	"	
Bond, Elisha	"	"	
Burnett, John	"	"	
Brown, Shearwood	"	"	
Burress, Elijah		"	On furlough.
Coffee, Thomas	Hamilton Co.	"	Absent on furlough.
Cannimore, Samuel		"	
Coons, Martin		"	One bay horse lost, valued at $53.
Davenport, James		"	Promoted June 16, 1832....[lost, valued at $67
Fouch, John		"	One bay horse, saddle, bridle and blanket
Hungate, Charles	Hamilton Co.	"	
Hall, Joseph		"	
Hutson, Sanford	"	"	Absent on furlough.
Hall, Thomas		"	One sorrel mare broke down, valued at $40.
Hanks, Thomas J.		"	
Johnston, Jesse		"	Discharged by Capt. Palmer on —— day.
Krisel, Charles	Hamilton Co.	"	One gun lost on battle ground, valued at $15.
Krisel, John	"	"	Absent on furlough.
Lane, Louis	"	"	
Lane, Levin	"	"	Promoted June 16, 1832, to Q. M.-Sergt.
Meredith, Frederick	"	"	Absent on furlough.
Monday, Samuel	"	"	
McBroom, Azahel	"	"	Absent on furlough.
McLaughlin, Wm.		"	
Morris, William		"	[valued at $71
Maulding, Ambrose		"	On furlough. One bay mare, etc., stolen,

FIRST BRIGADE.

Name and Rank.	Residence.	Enrolled	Remarks.
		1832.	
Oglesby, Rhebin	Hamilton Co.	June 16	Horse, saddle, etc., stolen by Indians; furloughed.
Overturf, Adam		"	
Phelps, Charles	Hamilton Co.	"	
Pauley, Alexander	"	"	
Perry, William		"	
Prigmore, Wilie		"	
Redrick, Jonathan	Hamilton Co.	"	Mare killed on forced march; valued at $63.
Rich, John	"	"	
Reynolds, Jeremiah		"	
Shealy, Moses	"	"	Mare, etc., stolen by Indians; valued at $94.
Schoolcraft, James		"	
Sims, Martin		"	[furloughed.
Townsand, Hiram	Hamilton Co.	"	Horse, saddle, etc., lost on forced march;
Tramel, Elijah	"	"	[loughed.
White, Snead	"	"	Mare, saddle, etc., stolen by Indians; fur-
Williams, Wiley	"	"	
Ward, Samuel	"	"	

I certify on honor that this muster roll exhibits true statement of the company under my command, and that the remarks set opposite the name of each officer and soldier are, to the best of my knowledge, accurate and just.
(Signed.) JAMES HALL, CAPT.,
Com. 1st Co., 2d Bat, 3d Regt., 1st Brig. Ill. Mounted Vol.

Mustered out of service by me, by order of Major-General Scott, commanding the N. W. army.
(Signed.) Z. C. PALMER, CAPT.,
6th U. S. Inft., Com. Post.

CAPT. JAMES N. CLARK'S COMPANY

Of 3d Regiment, 1st Brigade, Illinois Mounted Volunteers, called into the service of the United States on the requisition of Gen. Atkinson, by the Governor's proclamation dated May 15, 1832. Mustered out August 15, 1832.

Name and Rank.	Residence.	Enrolled	Remarks.
Captain.		1832.	
James N. Clark	Wayne Co.	June 16	Saddle, bridle and blanket lost
First Lieutenant.			
David Ray	"	"	One horse lost
Second Lieutenant.			
Jesse Laird	"	"	
Sergeants.			
Daniel Sumpter	"	"	On furlough August 10, 1832; lost saddle
William A. Howard	"	"	
Henry Oley	"	"	2d August, 1832, Ft. Dickson, to be discharged
Isaac Street	"	"	
Corporals.			
Joseph Walker	"	"	
John A. McWhartens	"	"	On furlough Aug. 3, 1832
Lewis Watkins	"	"	
Nathan E. Roberts	"	"	
Privates.			
Austin, Harris	"	"	
Austin, James B	"	"	
Alexander, David	"	"	Discharged at Ft. Dickson, Aug. 2, 1832
Bain, Robert	"	"	On furlough Aug. 9, 1832
Bradshaw, Greenup	"	"	
Bullard, Asa	"	"	
Campbell, Joseph M	"	"	Horse lost
Clark, James	"	"	
Clark, William [H	"	"	
Dickerson, Younger	"	"	
Dolton, George	"	"	
Dolton, Andrew C	"	"	

BLACK HAWK WAR.

Name and Rank.	Residence.	Enrolled	Remarks.
		1832.	
Farleigh, George	Wayne Co	June 16	
Fitzgerald, John F.	"	"	Furloughed Aug. 8, 1832
Garrison, Joseph L.	"	"	Left sick at Fort Wilbourn, June 19, 1832
Garrison, James	"	"	
Graham, William	"	"	
Hargrave, Jeremiah	"	"	
Harland, William	"	"	Furloughed August 9, 1832
Haws, Alfred	"	"	
Haws, Benjamin	"	"	
Hanson, John	"	"	Left at Fort Wilbourn, sick, June 19, 1832
James, Samuel	"	"	
Kenshalow, Peter	"	"	
Martin, David	"	"	
Martin, Nathan	"	"	
Mays, Andrew	"	"	
Mays, James	"	"	
McCullam, William	"	"	
Morris, Joseph	"	"	
Ray, Chesley	"	"	
Ray, Asa	"	"	
Rister, Jacob	"	"	Left at Fort Wilbourn, sick, June 19, 1832
Sanders, Fenton	"	"	
Sessions, Richard	"	"	
Slocumb, David D.	"	"	Discharged at Fort Wilbourn, June 19, 1832
Smith, David	"	"	
Trotter, James	"	"	
Tyler, Johnlen	"	"	On furlough Aug. 9, 1832
Walker, George	"	"	
Walker, Greenbury	"	"	
Warrick, Jefferson	"	"	
Warrick, James R.	"	"	
Widdus, John G.	"	"	On furlough Aug. 9, 1832
White, John L.	"	"	
Bradshaw, Arthur	"	"	

James N. Clark elected Captain, May 12, 1832. David Ray elected 1st Lieut., May 12. Jesse Laird elected 2d Lieut., May 12, 1832.

From Wayne county took up line on June 1, 1832. Mustered into service June 16, 1832.

Capt. Berryman G. Wells' Company

Of the 3d Regiment, 1st Brigade of Illinois Mounted Volunteers, called into the service of the United States, on the requisition of Gen. Atkinson, by the Governor's proclamation dated May 15, 1832. Mustered out August 15, 1832.

Name and Rank.	Residence.	Enrolled	Remarks.
		1832.	
Captain.			
Benjamin G. Wells	Wayne Co	June 16	
First Lieutenant.			
John Brown	"	"	On furlough from Aug. 7
Second Lieutenant.			
James B. Carter	"	"	
Sergeants.			
Hugh Stewart	"	"	Absent by leave of Col. Leech
James G. Browner	"	"	
Leon Harrys	"	"	Furloughed Aug. 9
Riley T. Serratt	"	"	
Corporals.			
Robert S. Harriss	"	"	Furloughed Aug. 9
Ransom Harriss	"	"	
Albert Butler	"	"	
Elijah Harriss	"	"	On furlough Aug. 9
Drummer.			
Nathan Franklin	"	"	On furlough Aug. 9

FIRST BRIGADE.

Name and Rank.	Residence.	Enrolled	Remarks.
Trumpeter.		1832.	
Jonathan Wilsey	Wayne Co	June 16	On furlough Aug. 9
Privates.			
Bird, John	"	"	
Beach, Justis	"	"	Absent by leave of Col. Leech
Browner, John	"	"	
Berry, John	"	"	
Cates, Robert D	"	"	
Cates, Robert	"	"	Horse, etc., lost
Cook, Howlet H	"	"	
Cook, James M	"	"	
Carter, Isaac	"	"	
Carter, William	"	"	Absent by leave of Col. Leech
Downer, Job	"	"	
Gasten, Robert R	"	"	
Hall, Jacob	"	"	Furloughed Aug. 9
Hodges, Isaih	"	"	
Hodges, Isham	"	"	Absent Aug. 3 by leave of Col. Leech
Harland, James C	"	"	" " " " " "
Hart, Moses	"	"	Furloughed Aug. 9
Harriss, Joseph	"	"	Absent on leave to Galena; taken sick; went
Irvin, William	"	"	Furloughed June 25.....[home without leave.
Lock, Samuel	"	"	Absent on furlough; one horse, etc., lost
McCracken, Jon'th'n	"	"	One horse, etc., lost
Martin, Nathan	"	"	Absent from Aug. 3 by leave of Col. Leech
Neel, Samuel	"	"	
Neel, Andrew	"	"	
Neel, Henry	"	"	One horse, etc., lost
Phelps, Thomas	"	"	Absent by leave Aug. 3; one horse, etc., lost.
Smith, Nicholas	"	"	" " " " of Col. Leech; one musket,
Stephenson, John G	"	"	Furloughed Aug. 9 ....[etc., lost in battle.
Shoemaker, Enoch	"	"	Absent by leave Aug. 3; one horse lost
Shoemaker, Hugh	"	"	
Stephenson, Job	"	"	
Snider, John W	"	"	Furloughed Aug. 9; one horse, etc., lost
Staton, Westley	"	"	Absent by leave of Col. Leech, Aug. 3
Turner, Fielding C	"	"	
Turner, James	"	"	
White, William	"	"	Horse, etc., lost
Wells, M. C	"	"	Absent on furlough Aug. 9
Young, Clement C	"	"	

Berryman G. Wells elected Captain, John Brown elected First Lieutenant, James B. Carter elected Second Lieutenant, May 12, 1832. Non-commissioned officers appointed same date.

SPY BATTALION.

Capt. William N. Dobbins' Company

Of Spy Battalion, 1st Brigade, of Illinois Mounted Volunteers, called into the service of the United States by the Governor's proclamation, dated April 19, 1832; mustered out August 16, 1832.

Name and Rank.	Residence.	Enrolled	Remarks.
Captain.		1832.	
William N. Dobbins	Marion Co...	June 16	Horse wounded, not fit for service; rifle lost.
First Lieutenant.			
Steven Yocum	" "	" "	Lost 1 U. S. halter
Second Lieutenant.			
James Gray	" "	" "	On furlough August 11; horse killed
Sergeants.			
John F. Draper	" "	" "	Absent by leave Aug. 11; lost 1 U. S. halter
Alfred Ray	" "	" "	
Samuel Hull	" "	" "	Absent by leave August 11
Daniel Mynes	" "	" "	
Corporals.			
Hamilton Farthing	" "	" "	Horse killed; lost 1 U. S. rope
William B. Haddem	" "	" "	Absent by leave August 11
William T. Booth	" "	" "	Lost 1 U. S. halter
Joseph Gray	" "	" "	Absent by leave Col. Leech; horse killed
Privates.			
Allen, Benjamin	" "	" "	Lost 1 U. S. halter
Allen, John	" "	" "	Absent on furlough August 12
Allman, David W	" "	" "	Absent by leave August 11; horse lost
Chandler, Wells	" "	" "	" " 11; " killed
Craig, William H	" "	" "	Disch.; must'd out by Lieut. Depriest Aug. 3.
Craig, Samuel	" "	" "	Discharged; horse wounded; lost U. S. halt'r
Dunken, Green R	" "	" "	" lost U. S. camp kettle
Eagan, John	" "	" "	
Farmer, William	" "	" "	
Fields, Green	" "	" "	Disch.; horse killed; lost 1 U. S. coffee pot
Field, Nathan	" "	" "	" lost 1 U. S. frying pan
Gaston, William	" "	" "	" horse killed; lost 1 U. S. coffee pot
Gray, William	" "	" "	
Hill, William	" "	" "	
Hollen, James	" "	" "	Absent by leave Aug. 11; lost 1 U. S. halter
Hutchison, Wm. G	" "	" "	Discharged
Hays, Samuel H	" "	" "	; horse killed
Jones, John F	" "	" "	Absent on furlough August 12
King, Willa	" "	" "	Discharged; lost 1 U. S. frying pan
King, William	" "	" "	" camp kettle; horse kill'd
Lovel, James	" "	" "	Absent by leave August 11; horse killed
Livenstone, Henry M	" "	" "	
McDaniel, Henry	" "	" "	Horse lost
McGuire, John	" "	" "	Lost 1 U. S. halter
McGee, William	" "	" "	
Mabry, Dudley H	" "	" "	Horse killed; rifle-gun lost; also, U. S. halter
Marsh, William	" "	" "	Absent by consent Gen. Atkinson Aug. 4
Nelms, Norflit B	" "	" "	" leave August 11; horse killed
Piles, Calven	" "	" "	Lost 1 U. S. halter; horse killed
Phelps, Zadock	" "	" "	
Phelps, John	" "	" "	Absent on furlough July 20
Richeson, James J	" "	" "	Lost 1 U. S. halter
Sterges, Jesse	" "	" "	Absent on furlough August 11
Smith, Wellers	" "	" "	Discharged; horse killed
Smith, John F	" "	" "	

FIRST BRIGADE.

Name and Rank.	Residence.	Enrolled	Remarks.
		1832.	
Tompson, Bird M....	Marion Co...	June 16.	Absent by leave Aug. 12; horse killed.........
Uhls, John B......	"	"	....
Williams, James....	"	"	Discharged; horse killed.............
Warren, Asa........	"	"	Absent by leave of Gen. Atkinson...........
Wright, Leven......	"	"	Absent on furl. Aug. 11; lost 1 U. S. halter;
Young, Edward......	"	"	Discharged; horse killed.......[horse killed.

Company was organized in Marion county May 4, 1832. Marched, June 1, for Fort Wilbourn. Mustered into service June 17, 1832. Fourteen horses killed in battle at Kellogg's Grove, six wounded and three taken by the enemy, June 25, 1832.

James Eagan,	left sick at Fort Wilbourn, to be discharged by Gen. Atkinson.				
Issac Coppall,	"	"	"	"	"
Wm. Howell,	"	"	"	"	"

I certify that Young Burbee, a private of my company, was detailed as Hospital Steward, and served out his full term, and was mustered out on the field and staff muster roll of the Spy Battalion.

(Signed.) WM. N. DOBBINS, CAPT.

CAPT. JAMES BOWMAN'S COMPANY

Of the Odd Battalion of Spies, 1st Brigade of Illinois Mounted Volunteers, called into the service of the United States, on the requisition of Gen. Atkinson, by the Governor's proclamation, dated May 15, 1832. Mustered out, Aug. 16, 1832.

Name and Rank.	Residence.	Enrolled	Remarks.
Captain.		1832	
James Bowman......	Jefferson Co..	June 17	....
First Lieutenant.			
Franklin S. Casey...	"	June 16	Furloughed Aug. 7, 1832.................
Second Lieutenant.			
Green Deprist......	"	"	Supposed to be furloughed Aug. 3, 1832........
Sergeants.			
Stephen C. Hicks...	"	"	Furloughed Aug. 17, 1832.............
Eli D. Anderson.....	"	"	Promoted 1st Serg't, *vice* Hicks, furloughed..
John R. Suterfield...	"	"	Supposed to be discharged August 12, 1832....
Littleton, Daniel.....	"	"	
Corporals.			
George Bullock......	"	"	....
James Bullock	"	"	
Isaac S. Casey.......	"	"	Furloughed August 7, 1832..................
Isaac Deprist	"	"	Supposed to be discharged August 3, 1832....
Privates.			
Anderson, H. S......	"	"	Promoted............................
Atchison, Wash'ton.	"	"	Supposed to be discharged August 3, 1832....
Atchison, Ignatius..	"	"	" " " "
Bingeman, William..	"	"	" " " "
Bradford, Joseph....	"	"	" " " "
Bruce, Marcus D. ...	"	"	" " " "
Buffington, Philip C.	"	"	" " " "
Baugh, John........	"	"	
Carpenter, Sam'l W.	"	"	
Casey, Zadock.......	"	"	Promoted and furloughed July 2, 1832.........
Darnall, John.......	"	"	Supposed to be discharged August 3, 1832 ...
Deweze, William....	"	"	
Elkin, Gazaway.....	"	"	....
Elkin, Robert.......	"	"	
Faulkenby, Isaac....	"	"	
Gastin, Wm. D......	"	"	Sick in tent...........................
Holder, Willis B.....	"	"	
Hays, William B.....	"	"	Furloughed Aug. 6, 1832................
Ham, James........	"	"	
Harlow, Joel........	"	"	
Isam, John..........	"	"	Furloughed Aug. 7, 1832................

Name and Rank.	Residence.	Enrolled	Remarks.
		1832.	
Kitrel, David	Jefferson Co.	June 16	Supposed to be discharged August 3, 1832
Martin, James C	"	"	" " " 12
Minor, James F	"	"	" " " 3
McBrien, John E	"	"	
Newby, Hezekiah	"	"	Supposed to be discharged August 12, 1832
Owens, Joshua	"	"	
Owens, Peter	"	"	" " "
Parish, Wiott	"	"	
Pace, George W	"	"	Furloughed July 10, 1832, to care for wounded
Rhea, James	"	"	
Reynolds, Jacob	"	"	Supposed discharged Aug. 12, 1832
Tarnison, William	"	"	Discharged Aug. 12, 1832

Dead:

		1832	
Allen, William	Jefferson Co.	June 16	Killed at Kellogg's Grove June 25
Black, James	"	"	
Band, James B	"	"	
Bradford, Abner	"	"	
Meek, Robert	"	"	Wounded (?)
Randolph, Marcus	"	"	Wounded at Kellogg's Grove; furl'd June 10.

I certify on honor that Zadock Casey volunteered in my company as a private, and proceeded to Fort Wilbourn, where, on June 17, 1832, he was promoted to Paymaster of the Spy Battalion, and served as such to the end of the Indian war. He is therefore entitled to traveling pay as a private to Wilbourn from this place.

(Signed.)   JAMES BOWMAN,
MOUNT VERNON, May 16, 1833.   late Captain.

Company organized May 28, 1832. Marched for Hennepin June 12, 1832.
12 horses killed at Kellogg's Grove, June 25, 1832.
8 wounded
5 missing   "   "
4 wounded   "   Recovered.

Mustered into service at Wilbourn June 17, 1832. Drew only one-half bushel corn per horse, since mustered into service. Drew only one ration per day for self since mustered into service. Furnished 8 days' rations each at Springfield.

DETACHMENT.

Capt. William S. Stephenson's Detachment

Of Illinois Mounted Volunteers, called into the service of the United States by the Governor of the State, by his order of May 15, 1832, from the date of its enrollment to the 3d day of August, 1832, when mustered out of service.

Name and Rank.	Residence.	Enrolled	Remarks.
First Lieutenant.		1832.	
James G. Corder	Franklin Co.	June 16	
Sergeant.			
Abraham Ray	" "	" "	
Corporals.			
James G. Trovillian	" "	" "	Horse killed in battle; saddle and bridle lost.
William Crawford	" "	" "	Horse lost; supposed stolen by Indians
Privates.			
England, William	" "	" "	
Flannagan, Jas. W.	" "	" "	Horse and saddle lost
Galloway, Robert	" "	" "	Horse shot in battle; saddle, bridle, etc., lost
Harrison, Benj. N.	" "	" "	Horse lost in battle; also saddle and bridle
Hutson, John	" "	" "	Horse shot in battle
Herold, Lewis	" "	" "	Horse killed in battle; saddle-bags, etc., lost
Ice, James			
Jones, Whitman	" "	" "	Horse killed in battle.
Kirkpatrick, William	" "	" "	
Kirkpatrick, Edward	" "	" "	
Mutton, Wilson L	" "	" "	
Newman, Clayton	" "	" "	
Piner, William	" "	" "	
Polk, John	" "	" "	Horse lost in battle; also saddle and bridle
Taylor, John	" "	" "	
Williams, Milton	" "	" "	Horse killed in battle; saddle, bridle, etc., lost

Capt. Charles Dunn's Company, Second Regiment, First Brigade, detached part thereof:

Name and Rank.	Residence.	Enrolled	Remarks.
Sergeants.		1832	
William T. Walters	Pope Co.	June 16	
James Modglin	" "	" "	
Samuel Roper	" "		
Corporal.			
Ransom King	" "	" "	
Privates.			
Barger, Abraham S.	" "	" "	
Crane, Elkin	" "	" "	
Cooper, David	" "	" "	
Dyke, John	" "	" "	
Fulkeson, James	" "	" "	
Lauderdale, William	" "	" "	Horse lost in service in forced march
Walters, Thomas, Jr.	" "	" "	
Walters, William H.	" "	" "	
Whiteside, William	" "	" "	

Capt. Russell's Company, First Regiment, First Brigade:

Name and Rank.	Residence.	Enrolled	Remarks.
Second Lieutenant. Edward Vinson	Gallatin Co.	1832. June 16	
Privates. Birchum, Joseph	"	"	Horse lost in service in forced march
Dunn, Isham	"	"	
Hill, Allen	"	"	
Hampton, David	"	"	
Wise, William	"	"	Horse lost in service in forced march

Capt. Arman's Company, Second Regiment, First Brigade:

Name and Rank.	Residence.	Enrolled	Remarks.
Corporals. Alexander McCorkle	Pope Co.	1832. June 16.	
Thomas W. Tanner	"	"	Mare lost in service in forced march
Bugler. John Castner	"	"	
Privates. Alexander, William	"	"	
Bennet, Richard	"	"	Mare and saddle lost in service
Bayles, William H.	"	"	Absent on furlough
Dyer, Joel	"	"	Horse rode down in forced march, and left
Holoman, James	"	"	Horse lost in service, and saddle left
McMurphy, John	"	"	
Tanner, John A	"	"	
Williams, William	"	"	Horse badly lamed in service, and left
Wallace, Sampson	"	"	

Capt. West's Company, Second Regiment, First Brigade:

Name and Rank.	Residence.	Enrolled	Remarks.
Sergeants. James Youngblood	Franklin Co.	1832. June 16.	
James Parker	"	"	
Corporals. Aaron Youngblood	"	"	
Martin Asbridge	"	"	
Obediah Rich	"	"	
Privates. Cane, John	"	"	
Finney, William	"	"	
Groves, William	"	"	
Gibbons, William	"	"	
Keaster, Lewis	"	"	
Keaster, George	"	"	
Murphy, John	"	"	
Welty, Jacob	"	"	Horse crippled in forced march; saddle left
Youngblood, Sol.	"	"	
Youngblood, Jon'th'n	"	"	

Capt. Holiday's Company, First Regiment, First Brigade:

Name and Rank.	Residence.	Enrolled	Remarks.
Private. Mason Wood	Gallatin Co.	1832. June 16	

Capt. Bowyer's Company, Second Regiment, First Brigade:

Name and Rank.	Residence.	Enrolled	Remarks.
Corporal. John Suleven	Franklin Co.	1832 June 16	
Sergeant. Elijah Estes	"	"	
Privates. Aikins, Walter L. Estes, John Hutson, Owen McClain, Aikin	" " " "	" " " "	

SECOND BRIGADE.

FIRST REGIMENT.

Capt. Thos. B. Ross' Company

1st Regiment, 2d Brigade, of Illinois Mounted Volunteers, called into the service of the United States, on the requisition of Gen. Atkinson, by the Governor's proclamation, dated May 15, 1832. Mustered out August 15, 1832, by order of Brig.-Gen. Atkinson.

Name and Rank.	Residence.	Enrolled	Remarks.
Captain.		1832.	
Thos. B. Ross............	Coles Co......	June 18	....
First Lieutenant.			
James Shaw............	"	"	....
Second Lieutenants.			
Isaac Lewis............	"	"	Resigned July 25, 1832..................................
Thomas Sconce........	"	"	Promoted 2d Lieutenant July 25, 1832............
Sergeants.			
James Shaw, 1st......	"	"	
Daniel Needham, 2d..	"	"	Horse lost in service.....................................
Thos. Barnham, 3d...	"	"	Furl. from Ft. Dickson Aug. 13; app. 3d Sergt.
Silas M. Parker, 3d..	"	"	Disch. f'm Ft. Coscanang on Surg. cer. July 19
Samuel Doty, 4th.....	"	"	....
Corporals.			[Coscanang.
Van S. Castin, 1st....	"	"	Sup. disch. under Capt. Brimberry; left at Ft.
James James, 2d.....	"	"	
John Barnham, 4th..	"	"	Furl. from Ft. Dickson Aug. 13; horse lost....
Privates.			
Austin, Nathan.......	"	"	....
Adams, John J........	"	"	....[Coscanang.
Ashman, Hezek'h N.	"	"	Sup. disch. under Capt. Brimberry; left at Ft.
Brown, James G.....	"	"	Furloughed June 22, 1832, from Ft. Wilbourn.
Barker, Thomas......	"	"	Prom. 3d Sergt. July 25; furl. Aug. 13, Ft. Wil.
Bracken, Jesse........	"	"	
Baker, Mark...........	"	"	Furloughed August 13 from Ft. Dickson......
Carrico, John..........	"	"	Left sick at Ft. Dickson ....
Canterbury, Reuben.	"	"	....[Coscanang.
Custin, Harman......	"	"	Sup. disch. under Capt. Brimberry; left at Ft.
Chadwell, John.......	"	"	" " " "
Duty, William.........	"	"	
Duty, Richard.........	"	"	
Easton, John W.......	"	"	Furloughed at Ft. Dickson August 13, 1832...
Frust, Samuel.........	"	"	Horse lost in service..................................
Frazier, William......	"	"	....[Coscanang.
Frost, Henry...........	"	"	Sup. disch. under Capt. Brimberry; left at Ft.
Gordon, Patrick.......	"	"	
Gastin, Gibson........	"	"	
Gately, John G........	Sangamon Co	"	" " " "
Hart, Jonathan........	Coles Co......	"	" " " "

SECOND BRIGADE.   29

Name and Rank.	Residence.	Enrolled	Remarks.
		1832.	
Halfhill, Abram	Coles Co	June 18	
Hays, Thomas	"	"	Lost 1 pistol in service, worth $5
Kellogg, Samuel	"	"	Disch. f'm Ft.Coseanang on Surg. cer. July 19
Lester, Segler H	"	"	[Coseanang.
Logan, William	"	"	Sup. disch. under Capt.[Brimberry; left at Ft.
Odell, Isaac	"	"	
Phelps, Chas. D	"	"	" " "
Parker, Nathaniel	"	"	" " "
Parker, Benj., Jr	"	"	
Parker, Jonathan	"	"	
Riley, Thomas	"	"	
Sluder, Thomas C	"	"	
Scott, Andrew	"	"	
Stone, James H	"	"	
Shin, T. G. M	"	"	
Vincent, Obediah	"	"	
Vanwinkle, Green L	"	"	
White, William M	"	"	
Waldrope, John	Clark Co	"	
Williams, Henry	Coles Co	"	
Williams, Horace	"	"	Sick; furl. from Ft. Wilbourn June 22, 1832
Waldrope, William	"	"	Furloughed from Kellogg's Grove Aug. 11
Woodall, David	"	"	" " Ft. Williams June 22
Young, John	"	"	

The company was organized and marched for the place of rendezvous on the 4th day of June, 1832. Drew one-half bushel corn per man, forage,|while in service. One bucket, one ax, one coffee pot, two tin cups, two frying pans, two tin pans, public property, lost while in service.

(Signed.)   THOS. B. ROSS, CAPT

N. B.—Two hundred and eighty rations have bee drawn for this company for traveling home from place of being mustered out of service.

(Signed.)   THOS. B. ROSS, CAPT.,

CAPT. SAMUEL BRIMBERRY'S COMPANY

1st Regiment, 2d Brigade of Illinois Mounted Volunteers, called into the service of the United States, on the requisition of Gen. Atkinson, by the Governor's proclamation dated May 15, 1832. Mustered out Aug. 15, 1832, by order of Brig.-Gen. Atkinson.

Name and Rank.	Residence.	Enrolled	Remarks.
First Lieutenant.		1832	
Philip B. Smith	Edgar Co	June 19	
Sergeants.			
James Adams	"	"	
William Craig	"	"	Ordered to Dixon; supposed mustered out
William Morgan	"	"	Absent by order Gen. Atkinson
John Morgan	"	"	Horse and equipage lost
Corporals.			
John Ripple, 1st	"	"	
John Young, 4th	"	"	
Privates.			
Anglin, Valentine	"	"	
Cronnick, Philip	"	"	
Crist, John	"	"	
Clapp, Joseph	"	"	
Charters, Duncan M	"	"	
Craig, Isaac N	"	"	Ordered to Dixon; supposed mustered out
Craig, Robert	"	"	" " "
Craig, Alexander	"	"	
Elledge, Isaac	"	"	Absent with leave; supposed mustered out
Ferrell, John	"	"	
Ferrell, William	"	"	
Goodman, William	"	"	
Grinder, Henderson	"	"	

Name and Rank.	Residence.	Enrolled	Remarks.
		1832.	
Henson, Robert	Edgar Co.	June 19	
Jones, Richard	"	"	
Jones, Thomas	"	"	Ordered to Dixon; supposed mustered out
Redmon, Greenbury	"	"	
Wells, Elijah	"	"	
Walls, James	"	"	
Williams, Samuel	"	"	Mare lost July 27, 1832
Wells, David A	"	"	

Moses Anglin and Joseph Andrews, privates of this company, were mustered into the service of the United States on the 19th day of June, 1832; mounted, armed and equipped, and on the 21st day of June were discharged by Brig.-Gen. Atkinson, being out of health. Their names were omitted on this muster roll by oversight, and they are fully entitled to pay to 21st of June, 1832.

(Signed.)   SAMUEL BRIMBERRY, Capt.,
                                   (Signed.)
                                     M. K. ALEXANDER,
                                     Brig.-Gen. 2d Brig. Ill. Mil.

N. B.—The officers and men of this company have drawn only one ration each per day, and one-half bushel of corn forage each, during the campaign, and rations were furnished by each individual from home to Hennepin, on the Illinois river.

N. B.—This company was organized on the 10th day of May, 1832, and started from Paris, Edgar county, on the 4th day of June, 1832, to Hennepin, to rendezvous there on the 10th, by the Governor's orders. From there ordered to Wilbourn to rendezvous, on the 15th day of June, 1832. On the 17th were formed into regiment. On the 18th of June formed into a brigade, and on the 19th day of June, 1832, mustered into service.

Drew 10 days' traveling rations.

Capt. Isaac Sanford's Company

1st Regt., 2d Brigade of Illinois Mounted Volunteers, called into the service of the United States, on the requisition of Gen. Atkinson, by the Governor's proclamation dated May 15, 1832. This company was organized, etc., in Edgar county, May 10, 1832. Mustered out August 15, 1832, by order of Brig.-Gen. Atkinson.

Name and Rank.	Residence.	Enrolled	Remarks.
Captain,		1832.	
Isaac Sanford	Edgar Co.	June 19	
First Lieutenant,			
William Runyan	"	"	
Second Lieutenant,			
Aloysius Brown	"	"	Furloughed Aug. 4, 1832
Sergeants.			
Thomas J. Buntain	"	"	
George G. Boord	"	"	Mare and equipage lost
Charles Bodine	"	"	
Alfred VanHoutan	"	"	Furloughed Aug. 4, 1832; lost his horse
Corporals.			
John D. Bozeith	"	"	July 21, 1832, ordered to Dixon's Ferry
John Smith	"	"	" " " "
Wineson Robertson	"	"	" " " "
James Cummings	"	"	Furloughed Aug. 4, 1832
Privates.			
Allen, Harding C.	"	"	
Buntain, Andrew E.	"	"	July 21, 1832, ordered to Dixon's Ferry
Breeden, Fielder	"	"	
Bradshaw, Elias	"	"	July 21, 1832, ordered to Dixon's Ferry
Boord, Mezaldue H.	"	"	" " " "
Chipps, George W.	"	"	
Cowan, John	"	"	
Camp, Abisha	"	"	Mare lost, lamed and rendered useless
Cummings, John	"	"	Furloughed Aug. 4, 1832

SECOND BRIGADE.

Name and Rank.	Residence.	Enrolled	Remarks.
		1832.	
Davis, Abraham	Edgar Co.	June 19	Left sick at Fort Coscanang, July 10, 1832
Drummond, Henry	"	"	
Davis, James	"	"	July 21, 1832, ordered to Dixon's Ferry
Ewing, James	"	"	July 21, 1832, ordered to Dixon's Ferry
Edwards, Allemus	"	"	July 21, 1832, ordered to Dixon's Ferry
Ewing, George	"	"	
Furnish, Thomas	"	"	July 21, 1832, ordered to Dixon's Ferry
Foster, Arthur	"	"	Furloughed Aug. 4, 1832
Foster, John	"	"	July 21, 1832, ordered to Dixon's Ferry
Fuller, John	"	"	
Gillepey, James	"	"	" " "
Harding, George	"	"	
Hunter, Andrew	"	"	July 21, 1832, ordered to Dixon's Ferry
Hollingsworth, John	"	"	Lost one pistol, appraised at $3
Hunsacker, Benj'min	"	"	Furloughed Aug. 9, 1832
Hill, John	"	"	
Hawkins, James	"	"	
Hunter, Spencer R.	"	"	Sick
Jourdan, Hartwell	"	"	
Kehoe, Young	"	"	
Knight, John	"	"	
Knight, Joseph	"	"	
Lowery, Jacob D.	"	"	
Lewis, William	"	"	
Martin, Chas. K.	"	"	
Murphy, W. C.	"	"	July 21, 1832, ordered to Dixon's Ferry
McIntire, Lucius	"	"	Furloughed Aug. 4, 1832
McCully, Henry	"	"	
Montgomery, Wm.	"	"	
Morrison, David	"	"	
Martain, John	"	"	Name omit'd on original roll; on duty f'm start
Macy, Samuel	"	"	
Nolle, Thomas	"	"	July 21, 1832, ordered to Dixon's Ferry
Townall, George C.	"	"	
Percell, James C.	"	"	Furloughed Aug. 4, 1832; lost horse and gun
Percell, Edward	"	"	
Ray, Martain	"	"	Furloughed Aug., 1832
Ray, Isaac	"	"	
Ray, Jesse	"	"	July 21, 1832, ordered to Dixon's Ferry
Ray, James	"	"	
Ray, William	"	"	Left at Dixon's Ferry, June 25, 1832
Ross, William	"	"	July 21, 1832, ordered to Dixon's Ferry
Roed, George	"	"	
Reed, William	"	"	
Ripple, Daniel	"	"	
Ripple, Michael	"	"	
Stump, Francis	"	"	
Taylor, Joseph	"	"	
Taylor, Gabril N.	"	"	
Ferrill, John	"	"	
VanHoutan, Isaac	"	"	
VanHoutan, Wm.	"	"	
Wilson, Larkin	"	"	
Wilson, Reason	"	"	

Record of events which may be necessary or useful for future reference at the War Department, or for present information:

N. B.—This company was organized on the 10th day of May, 1832, and started from Paris, Edgar county, on the 4th day of June, 1832, to Hennepin, to rendezvous there on the 10th, by the Governor's orders. From thence ordered to Wilbourn to rendezvous on the 15th day of June, 1832; on the 17th of June were formed into regiments; on the 18th of June formed into a brigade, and on the 19th day of June, 1832, mustered into service of the United States.

Rations have been drawn for the company at this place to return home, viz: Ten days, up to and including 25th day of August, 1832. I also believe, by information, that those men ordered to Dixon's are discharged under Capt. Brimberry.

Received, also, of the United States, 11 halters, 4 tent cloths; 3 of the best cloths have been returned, the other tent worn out or lost. All the halters worn out or lost.

All of which I certify on honor, at Dixon's Ferry, August 15, 1832.

    (Signed.)   ISAAC SANFORD.

The officers and men of the company have drawn only one ration each per day, and one-half bushel corn forage each, during the campaign, and rations were furnished by each individual from home to Hennepin, on the Illinois river. All of which I certify on honor the 15th day of August, 1832.

    (Signed.)   ISAAC SANFORD, Capt.

Capt. Robert Griffin's Company

Of the 1st Regiment, 2d Brigade, Illinois Mounted Volunteers, army of the United States, called into the service of the United States, on the requisition of Gen. Atkinson, by the Governor's proclamation, dated 1832; mustered out August 15, 1832, by order of Brig.-Gen. Atkinson.

Name and Rank.	Residence.	Enrolled	Remarks.
Captain.		1832.	
Robert Griffin	Edgar Co.	June 19	Two buckets, ax, tub, lost, Mud Lake to Dixon
First Lieutenant.			
George Moke	"	"	One halter lost on the march.
Second Lieutenant.			
Wm. N. Redman	"	"	Detailed to Dixon; supposed to be discharged
Sergeants.			
Jesse Raper	"	"	
George Phillips	"	"	Detailed to Dixon; supposed to be discharged
Edmund Minor	"	"	Absent with leave
George Redman	"	"	supposed to be discharged
Corporals.			
James McCoy	"	"	
Wm. P. Hicklin	"	"	Absent with leave; 1 horse lost
Wm. H. Faulkner	"	"	
Addison M. Qurvy	"	"	Absent with leave; supposed to be discharged
Privates.			
Alexander, Edmund	"	"	Absent without leave; supposed discharged.
Bryant, William	"	"	
Craig, John	"	"	Horse and equipments lost at Ft. Wilbourn.
Coe, James	Vermilion Co.	"	Detailed to Dixon; supposed to be discharged
Clapp, Levi	Edgar Co.	"	
Darnal, Wm	"	"	Horse, etc., lost; disch. on Surgeon's certif.
Downs, Abraham	"	"	Absent without leave.
Davis, Samuel	"	"	Furloughed August 13, 1832.
Dick, Ferdinand	"	"	Detailed to Dixon; supposed to be discharged
Elledge, William	"	"	Ft. Hamilton to hunt horses
Flood, William	"	"	
Fears, William	"	"	One camp kettle lost on forced march
Flack, James	"	"	Furlough
Furness, John	"	"	Detailed to Dixon; 1 horse lost
Green, William	"	"	
Harbaugh, Jacob	"	"	
Hensley, George W.	"	"	Equipage lost
Jones, Thomas	"	"	Absent without leave; supposed discharged.
Lacksu, Tobias J.	"	"	
Lamb, Arthur	"	"	
May, William	"	"	Horse and equipage lost
Martin, Moses	"	"	Left at Fort Wilbourn, sick
Nobles, Jonathan B.	"	"	
Owsley, Henry	"	"	
Patterson, Jonathan	"	"	Detailed to Ft. Dixon; 1 horse, etc., lost
Packet, John	"	"	Dixon; supposed to be discharged
Parish, James	"	"	
Rockhold, Ezekiel	"	"	Horses and equipage lost
Stewart, Joseph H.	"	"	Detailed to Dixon; supposed to be discharged
Sizemon, Martin	"	"	Absent without leave
Southerland, R. B.	"	"	
Snyder, William	"	"	Horse and equipage lost
Smith, Samuel	"	"	
Tennery, Isaac H.	"	"	
Tennery, Patrick C.	"	"	
Thompson, John S.	"	"	Absent without leave.
Tade, John	"	"	Detailed to Dixon; supposed to be discharged
Wayne, George W.	"	"	
Wright, Joseph	"	"	

N. B.—This company was organized on the 10th day of May, 1832, and started from Paris, Edgar county, on the 4th day of June, 1832, to Hennepin, to rendezvous there on the 10th, by the Governor's orders. From thence, ordered to Wilbourn, to rendezvous there on the 15th of June, 1832. On the 17th of June, were formed into Regiments. On the 18th of June, formed into Brigades; and, on the 19th day of June, 1832, mustered into service. Drew ten days' traveling rations.

N. B.—The officers and men of this company have drawn only one ration each per day, and one-half bushel of corn forage, each, during the campaign; and rations were furnished by each individual from home to Hennepin, on the Illinois river.

Capt. Jonathan Mayo's Company

Of the 1st Regiment, 2d Brigade, of Illinois Mounted Volunteers, called into the service of the United States, on the requisition of Gen. Atkinson, by the Governor's proclamation, dated ——, 1832; mustered out August 15, 1832, by order of Brig.-Gen. Atkinson.

Name and Rank.	Residence.	Enrolled	Remarks.
Captain.		1832.	
Jonathan Mayo	Edgar Co.	June 19.	
First Lieutenant.			
Edward Y. Russell	"	"	Absent with leave, Aug. 4, 1832.
Second Lieutenant.			
John S. McConkey	"	"	
Sergeants.			
James Buchannon	"	"	Appointed 1st Sergeant June 19, 1832
David Crozier	"	"	
Daniel Spencer	"	"	Horse lost.
Joseph G. Barkley	"	"	Appointed 4th Sergeant June 19, 1832.
Corporals.			
Simon Cameron	"	"	
Tracy Wheeler	"	"	
James Bailey	"	"	Ordered to Dixon's; supposed discharged.
William N. Shaw	"	"	Appointed 4th Corporal June 19, 1832
Privates.			
Alexander, Wash'ton	"	"	
Bradley, John C.	"	"	Horse lost.
Burch, Newell	"	"	Supposed to be discharged; horse lost.
Bond, William	"	"	" " " ; two horses lost.
Bassford, Jonath'n S	"	"	Supposed to be discharged.
Certer, Willard	"	"	
Dezar, George	"	"	
Dill, John	"	"	
Dill, Milton M.	"	"	Supposed to be discharged
Doughertee, Thos. H	"	"	
Elder, Hugh M.	"	"	
Evans, Thomas	"	"	
Huff, Calvin H.	"	"	Absent with leave July 8, 1832.
Hobbs, Thomas	"	"	" " " Aug. 4, 1832
Hobbs, Enos	"	"	
Jones, Samuel	"	"	
Lowry, Reuben	"	"	Horse lost.
Lycan, Jacob J.	"	"	
Morgan, Wells	"	"	
Martin, Enos	"	"	
Morgan, Thomas	"	"	
Montgomera, Alex.	"	"	Supposed to be discharged
Matthews, John	"	"	
Pence, Emanuel	"	"	
Phillips, William	"	"	
Penson, Thomas	"	"	Absent with leave Aug. 4, 1832.
Rhea, Robert M.	"	"	
Rice, Hawkins	"	"	
Rice, Lewis	"	"	
Scott, Daniel	"	"	
Summerville, John	"	"	
Sprague, Harrison	"	"	Supposed to be discharged
Scott, Matthew R.	"	"	
Scott, Joseph	"	"	
Sumpter, Alexander	"	"	Horse lost.
Sumpter, Abraham	"	"	Supposed to be discharged; horse lost
Trimble, Green C.	"	"	
Vance, William B.	"	"	
Vance, Joseph	"	"	
Wilson, John	"	"	Horse lost.
Wyatt, Augustus B.	"	"	
Welch, Isaiah	"	"	Rifle bursted.
Welch, Abraham	"	"	
Whalen, Patrick	"	"	Absent with leave, Aug. 4, 1832.
Whitley, William	"	"	Transferred; appointed Hosp. Stew'd June 19

Resigned:

Name and Rank.	Residence.	Enrolled	Remarks.
First Sergeant, Parker, Leonard B.	Edgar Co.	1832. June 19	Appointed Quartermaster June 19, 1832

The officers and men of this company have drawn only one ration each per day, and one-half bushel of corn forage each during the campaign, and rations were furnished by each individual from Edgar county to Hennepin.

(Signed.)   J. MAYO, CAPT.

This company was organized at Paris, Edgar county, on the 10th day of May, 1832; took up the line of march for Hennepin on the 4th of June, the place where it was ordered to rendezvous, and reached that place on the 11th of June, and was mustered into the United States service at Wilbourn on June 19, 1832.

Ten days' rations are required, 8 drawn, 2 to be drawn.

(Signed.)   J. MAYO, CAPT.

William Whitley served till the 19th of July, when he engaged in the wagon train. He is entitled to pay till July 19, 1832.

(Signed.)   J. MAYO, CAPT.

CAPT. ROYAL A. NOTT'S COMPANY

Of the 1st Regiment, 2d Brigade, of Illinois Mounted Volunteers, called into the service of the United States, on the requisition of General Atkinson, by the Governor's proclamation, dated 15th of May, 1832. This company was organized in Clark county, May 31, 1832. Mustered out August 15, 1832, by order of Brig.-Gen. Atkinson.

Name and Rank.	Residence.	Enrolled	Remarks.
Captain, Royal A. Nott	Clark Co	1832. June 19	
First Lieutenant, Daniel Poorman	"	"	
Second Lieutenant, George W. Young	"	"	July 21, 1832, ord'd to Dixon's; disch.; lost mare
Sergeants.			
Stephen Archer	"	"	
John Fears	"	"	
James Lockard	"	"	
Oliver C. Lawwill	"	"	
Corporals.			
William T. McClure	"	"	
James Dunlap	"	"	
Noah Beauchamp	"	"	July 21, 1832, ordered to Dixon's; since disch
John W. Thompson	"	"	Lost sorrel mare, saddle, bridle and blanket
Privates.			
Archer, Jesse K.	"	"	
Boone, Daniel	"	"	Lost horse; strayed away
Burk, Samuel	"	"	Lost horse; ordered to Dixon's; since disch
Bostick, William	"	"	
Berry, George	"	"	
Bennett, Thomas F.	"	"	Lost his horse
Cooper, Theophelos	"	"	
Cowen, Joel	"	"	
Cooper, Chalkley I.	"	"	July 21, 1832, ord'd to Dixon's; disch.; lost mare
Crip, Jeremiah	"	"	
Chenowith, Martin L.	"	"	
DeHart, Alex. H.	"	"	July 21, 1832, ordered to Dixon's; discharged
DeHart, Lorenzo D.	"	"	
Davis, Alhanan H.	"	"	Lost his mare
Davis, Daniel	"	"	
Dolsen, Samuel	"	"	Furloughed at Prairie du Chien Aug. 9, 1832
Fleming, Andrew	"	"	July 21, 1832, ordered to Dixon's; discharged
Fanin, Ahalis	"	"	Horse worn out and left at Dixon's Ferry
Fears, Phineas	"	"	Lost his blanket

SECOND BRIGADE.

Name and Rank.	Residence.	Enrolled	Remarks.
		1832.	
Grove, Martin	Clark Co	June 19.	
Grant, John B.	"	"	
Henderson, James E.	"	"	
Henderson, Hez. A.	"	"	
Johnson, Saudford	"	"	
Kenny, Moses	"	"	July 21, 1832, ordered to Dixon's Ferry; disch.
Lafferty, Marshall	"	"	
Lathrop, Artemus	"	"	
McCabe, William	"	"	
McCabe, John	"	"	
McGuire, John	"	"	
Minor, Thomas	"	"	
Ogden, Benjamin	"	"	Sick and furloughed June 21, 1832
Ogden, Nehemiah	"	"	
Peters, Absalom O.	"	"	
Poorman, Samuel	"	"	July 21, 1832, ordered to Dixon's Ferry; disch.
Prero, Samuel	"	"	Furloughed at Prairie du Chien Aug. 7, 1832
Prero, Ira	"	"	
Payne, Ebenezer	"	"	July 21, 1832, ordered to Dixon's Ferry; disch.
Squires, Lyman R.	"	"	
Sharp, Elon	"	"	Lost his blanket
Shaw, James	"	"	
Stafford, Elijah	"	"	July 21, 1832, ordered to Dixon's Ferry; disch.
VanWinkle, John	"	"	Lost his blanket
Waters, John	"	"	Lost his horse
Wade, Thomas	"	"	
White, Thomas	"	"	Left his mare, etc., at Dixon's Ferry

This company of Volunteers assembled in Darwin, Clark county, Illinois, on the 31st day of May, 1832, and then and there elected officers, and from that place marched on the third day of June, 1832, and under the Governor's order rendezvoused at Hennepin, on the Illinois river, 11th day of June; next day marched and arrived at Fort Wilbourne, Lower Rapid, Illinois river, and the company was mustered into the United States service on the 19th day of said month of June, 1832. Rations have been drawn for the company at this place to return home, to-wit: fourteen days, up to and including the 28th day of August, 1832.

       (Signed.)   ROYAL A. NOTT, Capt.

August 15, 1832.

This company's officers and men have drawn one ration of provisions each per day only, and one peck of corn forage for horses each, and no more, during the campaign, and each individual furnished his own rations from home to Hennepin, on the Illinois river.

All of which I certify on honor.

       (Signed.)   ROYAL A. NOTT,
August 15, 1832.   Commanding the Company.

SECOND REGIMENT.

Capt. Alex. M. Houston's Company

Of the 2d Regiment, 2d Brigade, of Illinois Mounted Volunteers, called into the service of the United States, on the requisition of Gen. Atkinson, by the Governor's proclamation, dated May 15, 1832. Mustered out August 15, 1832, by order of Brig.-Gen. Atkinson.

Name and Rank.	Residence.	Enrolled	Remarks.
Captain.		1832.	
Alex M. Houston	Crawford Co.	June 19	
First Lieutenant.			
Geo. W. Lagon	" "	" "	Leave of absence by Gen. Atkinson; Aug. 4..
Second Lieutenant.			
James Boatright	" "	" "	
Sergeants.			[Dixon, July 10; sup. furl.
O. F. D. Hampton	" "	" "	Ord. on command with baggage wagon to Ft.
Levi Harper	" "	" "	Leave of absence from Ft. Hamilton, Aug. 4.
David Porter	" "	" "	
James Cristy	" "	" "	
Corporals.			[smith's Co.; discharged.
Cornelius Doherty	" "	" "	Ord. to Ft. Dixon; sup. att'ch'd to Capt. High-
James F. Stark	" "	" "	.......[smith's Co; discharged.
Joseph Jones	" "	" "	Ord. to Ft. Dixon; sup. att'ch'd to Capt. High-
Rivers Heath	" "	" "	Furl. Ft. Wilbourn, return home, sick, June 21
Bugler.			
Francis Waldrop	" "	" "	
Privates.			[smith's Co.; discharged.
Baugher, Geo. W.	" "	" "	Ord. to Ft. Dixon; sup. att'ch'd to Capt. High-
Brathares, Blanton	" "	" "	Furl. from Ft. Crawford to go home; app'ted
Bogard, John	" "	" "	..........[Corporal June 25.
Baker, Andrew	" "	" "	
Boatright, Alex	" "	" "	Furl. at Ft. Hamilton, to go home, Aug. 1
Cruse, Samuel	" "	" "	
Danforth, Silas L.	" "	" "	Furl. at Ft. Hamilton, to go home. Aug. 4
Doughton, Geo. R.	" "	" "	Ord. to Ft. Dixon; sup. att'ch'd to Capt. High-
Fitch, Edwin	" "	" "	..........[smith's Co.; discharged.
Fowler, Henry	" "	" "	
Goodwin, John	" "	" "	
Goodwin, Silas	" "	" "	
Grinton, Robert	" "	" "	
Hutton, John	" "	" "	..............[smith's Co.; discharged.
Hackett, Joseph	" "	" "	Ord. to Ft. Dixon; sup. att'ch'd to Capt. High-
Hackett, John A.	" "	" "	App. Q. M. Sergt. July 10....[smith's Co.; dis.
Hawkins, William	" "	" "	Ord. to Ft. Dixon; sup. att'ch'd to Capt. High-
Houne, John	" "	" "	Absented himself July 6, 1832
Kitchell, Wickliffe	" "	" "	Furl. to return home, July 10, at Ft. Cosgrum,
Kuykendall, James	" "	" "	...............[Dixon July 10; sup. furl.
Logan, Alex	" "	" "	Ord. on command with baggage wagon to Ft.
Lackey, Matthew	" "	" "	Absented himself July 6....[smith's Co.; dis.
McCoy, John	" "	" "	Ord. to Ft. Dixon; sup. att'ch'd to Capt. High-
Nelly, Johnson	" "	" "	
Porter, Robert	" "	" "	
Potter, Wm	" "	" "	..............[smith's Co.; discharged.
Pearson, Wm	" "	" "	Ord. to Ft. Dixon; sup. att'ch'd to Capt. High-
Pearson, Joseph	" "	" "	
Pearson, Edwin	" "	" "	" " " " " "
Phelps, Zalmon	" "	" "	

SECOND BRIGADE.

Name and Rank.	Residence.	Enrolled	Remarks.
		1832.	
Shaw, Samuel			Furl. at Ft. Dodge, to return home, Aug. 9
Stewart, John			[smith's Co.; discharged.
Vandeventer, Jno. F.			Ord. to Ft. Dixon; sup. att'ch'd to Capt. High-
Wilson, Vastin			Prom. Q. M. Sergt. June 29; ord. on command
Walters, Jacob			[with baggage wagons; sup. dis.

Organized the 12th of May, 1832; marched from home on the 2d day of June, by order; mustered into service June 19, 1832; drew two days' rations from the 16th inst.; forage drawn during service, one-half bushel corn for each horse; officers drew one ration each.

CAPT. JOHN ARNOLD'S COMPANY

Of the 2d Regiment of the 2d Brigade of Illinois Volunteers, called into the service of the United States, on the requisition of Gen. Atkinson, by the Governor's proclamation dated May 15, 1832. Mustered out August 15, 1832. This company was organized in Wabash county, May 12, 1832.

Name and Rank.	Residence.	Enrolled	Remarks.
Captain.		1832.	
James Arnold	Wabash Co.	June 19	
First Lieutenant.			
George Danforth	"	"	
Second Lieutenant.			
Samuel Fisher	"	"	Absent with leave
Sergeants.			
Mitchel C. Minnis	"	"	
Hiram Couch	"	"	
Mathias Leatherland	"	"	Absent with leave
John A. Dodds	"	"	" " " lost mare; appraised at $50
Corporals.			
Solomon Frear	"	"	Absent with leave
John Golden	"	"	" " "
Ira Keen	"	"	" " "
Wesley Woods	"	"	" " "
Privates.			
Besley, James	"	"	Absent with leave
Bass, Dolphin	"	"	
Buchannan, John W.	"	"	
Buchannan, Jos. O.	"	"	Absent with leave
Buchannan, Henry R.	"	"	" " " lost mare; appraised at $52
Brines, Jefferson	"	"	
Dodds, Joseph M.	"	"	Absent with leave
Godda, John	"	"	
Garner, James	"	"	" " " lost horse; appraised at $60
Golden, William	"	"	
Hull, Philip	"	"	
Hoyt, Jonathan S.	"	"	Absent with leave
Hobbert, Henry	"	"	
Keen, Dennis	"	"	
Miller, Barton S.	"	"	Absent with leave
McMillen, James	"	"	
Ochletree, John	"	"	" " "
Parmeter, Isaac	"	"	
Pixley, Isaac	"	"	
Ridgely, William	"	"	Absent with leave
Reel, Henry R.	"	"	" " " lost mare; appraised at $50
Sanford, Thomas	"	"	
Sanford, Jacob	"	"	
Smith, John O.	"	"	Absent with leave
Turner, Abner	"	"	" " " lost mare; appraised at $65
Utter, John	"	"	" " "
Vanderhoof, Philip	"	"	
Woods, Jeremiah	"	"	

Name and Rank.	Residence.	Enrolled	Remarks.
		1832.	
Wear, Thomas	Wabash Co.	June 19.	Absent with leave
Wear, Harvey	" "	" "	
Winders, Warren	" "	" "	
Wright, Robbert	" "	" "	

N. B.—The absentees are supposed to have been mustered out of service at Fort Dickson, under Capt. Jordan.

DETACHMENT OF CAPT. ELIAS JORDAN'S COMPANY

Of the 2d Regiment, 2d Brigade, of Illinois Mounted Volunteers, called into the service of the United States, on the requisition of Gen. Atkinson, by the Governor's proclamation dated May 15, 1832. The company was organized in Wabash county, May 12, 1832. Mustered out August 15, 1832. Enlisted for 90 days.

Name and Rank.	Residence.	Enrolled	Remarks.
First Lieutenant.		1832.	
James Kennerly	Wabash Co.		
Second Lieutenant.			
John N. Barnett	" "		On furlough Aug. 7.
Sergeant.			
James Grayson, 4th.	" "		
Corporal.			
Zach. Wilson, 2d	" "		On furlough Aug. 7.
Privates.			
Barnett, Benj. F.	" "		
Carlton, Robt.	" "		
Campbell, Robert	" "		
Campbell, Patrick S.	" "		
Fortney, Daniel	" "		On furlough Aug. 7, and horse lost.
Grayson, Wm.	" "		
Hood, Albert	" "		On furlough Aug. 7.
Levellett, Joseph	" "		
Painter, Joseph	" "		
Summer, Thomas	" "		
Summer, Joseph	" "		

DETACHMENT OF CAPT. HIGHSMITH'S COMPANY,

Organized May 1, 1832. Mustered out August 15, 1832.

Name and Rank.	Residence.	Enrolled	Remarks.
Sergeants.		1832.	
Beverly B. Piper, 1st	Crawford Co.		Elected 1st Sergeant June 22, 1832
John A. Christy, 4th	" "		
Corporal.			
Jackson James, 3d	" "		Elected 3d Corporal June 23, 1832
Privates.			
Attison, David M.	" "		
Barrick, John	" "		
Condrey, James	" "		
Gregg, John	" "		

SECOND BRIGADE.

Name and Rank.	Residence.	Enrolled	Remarks.
		1832.	
Grise, Wm. R.	Crawford Co.		
Johnson, Hiram	"		
Levitt, William	"		
Myers, John L.	"		
Myers, Andrew W.	"		
Parker, John, Sr.	"		
Parker, Wm	"		
Simons, Robert	"		
Vaunrinch, Jacob	"		

I certify that Jason D. Jones was mustered into the service of the United States in my company on June 19, 1832, and was honorably discharged from the service by Gen. Atkinson, on June 20 or 21. His name was omitted from the muster-roll by oversight.

(Signed.)   ELIAS JORDAN, Capt.

Mustered into service June 19, 1832.

DETACHMENT OF CAPT. BARNS' COMPANY

Of 2d Regiment, 2d Brigade of Illinois Mounted Volunteers, called into the service of the United States on the requisition of Gen. Atkinson, by the Governor's proclamation dated May 15, 1832. This company was organized in Lawrence county, Illinois, May 5, 1832. Mustered out August 15, 1832.

Name and Rank.	Residence.	Enrolled	Remarks.
		1832.	
Second Lieutenant.			
Daniel Morris	Lawrence Co.	June 19	Lost horse, reduced, worn out and left
Sergeants.			
John L. Bass, 1st	"	"	
Tho. McDonald, 2d	"	"	Lost horse, etc.; furloughed Aug. 7
Corporal.			
Jas. Buchanan, 2d	"	"	
Privates.			
Berton, Archibald	"	"	
Bass, Richard	"	"	
Crews, James	"	"	
Christy, Joseph R.	"	"	Furl. Aug. 2, to return with wounded men
Dunlap, Samuel	"	"	Promoted Adjutant July 9
Gallaher, Bonapart.	"	"	On extra duty at Beaughonan June 19
Gaddy, James	"	"	
Livingstone, John	"	"	
Moor, Edward	"	"	
Montgomery, John	"	"	Horse lost
Moaler, Peyton	"	"	Lost horse and equipage, and furloughed
McCleave, Benjamin	"	"	
Organ, Daniel	"	"	Lost mare; furl.; since disch'd; supposed to [be must'd out under Capt. Highsmith
Lewis, Thomas T.	"	"	
Pollard, James W.	"	"	
Richards, Joshua	"	"	
Turner, Thomas I.	"	"	
Turner, John	"	"	
Turner, E. D. M.	"	"	
Taylor, George W.	"	"	
Walden, John	"	"	

This company was organized in Lawrence county, Illinois, on May 5, 1832. Marched from there June 2, 1832. Arrived at Springfield June 9. Mustered into U. S. service June 19, 1832.

THIRD REGIMENT.

Capt. Solomon Hunter's Company

Of 3d Regiment, 2d Brigade of Illinois Mounted Volunteers, called into the service of the United States, on the requisition of Gen. Atkinson, by the Governor's proclamation dated May 15, 1832. This company was organized in the county of Edwards May 5, 1832. Mustered out Aug. 15, 1832, by order of Brig.-Gen. Atkinson.

Name and Rank.	Residence.	Enrolled	Remarks.
Captain,		1832.	
Solomon Hunter	Edwards Co.	June 19	Sword broke and lost in service
First Lieutenant,			
William Carrabaugh	"	"	
Second Lieutenant,			
John S. Rotrammel	"	"	
Sergeants.			
Thomas Jaggers	"	"	Ordered to Dixon's Ferry July 21, '32; disch'd
Joseph McCreary	"	"	Left sick at Ft. Wilbourn June 20, 1832
John Hocking	"	"	
John Brown	"	"	Ordered to Dixon's Ferry July 21, '32; disch'd
Corporals.			
William H. Harper	"	"	
Zach. Bottinghouse	"	"	Furloughed Aug. 7, 1832
Hugh Mounts	"	"	
James N. Harper	"	"	Ordered to Dixon's Ferry July 21, '32; disch'd
Privates.			
Bottinghouse, Dani'l	"	"	Left sick at Fort Wilbourn, June 20, 1832
Birkett, Thomas	"	"	
Batson, William	"	"	Ordered to Dixon's Ferry July 21, '32; disch'd
Birkett, Samuel	"	"	
Charles, Solomon	"	"	Ord'd to Dixon's July 21, 32; disch'd; lost mare
Case, John	"	"	
Curtis, George	"	"	Ordered to Dixon's Ferry July 21, '32; disch'd
Chism, Elisha	"	"	
Dodd, Milton	"	"	Ordered to Dixon's Ferry July 21, '32; disch'd
Dorothy, Robert	"	"	
Everly, Nimrod	"	"	Ordered to Ft. Wilbourn June 25, '32; disch'd
Emmerson, Alan	"	"	Promoted to Sergeant June 20, 1832
Fortner, John	"	"	Left sick at Fort Wilbourn, June 20, 1832
Fortner, Henry	"	"	Left on foot at Ft. Wilbourn June 20, 1832
Frazer, Hiram	"	"	
Hamilton, William	"	"	Furloughed Aug. 7, 1832
Hensley, Charles	"	"	Left sick at Fort Wilbourn June 21, 1832
Hobson, Dison	"	"	Ordered to Dixon's July 21, 1832; since disch'd
Jones, William E.	"	"	
Jennings, James	"	"	
McKinney, William	"	"	Ordered to Dixon's Ferry July 21, 32; disch'd
McCrackin, Hugh	"	"	Left sick at Fort Wilbourn June 20, 1832
Mebrose, William	"	"	Furloughed Aug. 4, 1832
Michels, Sumner	"	"	
Morris, Miles	"	"	Ordered to Dixon's July 6; disch'd; lost mare
Morris, George	"	"	" " " " " horse
Mifflin, William	"	"	" " " " since discharged.
Moss, Moses	"	"	Furloughed August 4, 1832
Rice Mathew	"	"	
Robinson, John G.	"	"	Ordered to Dixon's July 21; disch'd; lost horse
Snell, William	"	"	
Skinner, Thomas W.	"	"	Ordered to Dixon)s July 21, '32; since disch'd
Truscott, William	"	"	
Thompson, Francis D	"	"	Furloughed July 15, 1832

SECOND BRIGADE.   41

Name and Rank.	Residence.	Enrolled	Remarks.
		1832	
Tait, John............	Edwards Co..	June 19	Ordered to Dixon's July 21, 1832; since disch'd
Vincent, James......	"	"	Disch'd at Ft. Wilbourn June 20, '32; disability
Vincent, Josiah......	"	"	Ordered to Dixon's July 6, 1832; since disch..
Williams, Jonathan .	"	"	Left sick at Fort Wilbourn July 20, 1832........

The above named men ordered to Dixon's Ferry are said to have been discharged under Capt. E. Jordan.

This company was organized in Edwards county on the fifth day of May, 1832. Marched, according to Governor's order, for Hennepin, June 1, 1832. Was mustered into the service of the United States on the 19th of June, 1832. Each man of the company furnished six days' rations for himself and horse. The officers of said company drew one ration per day in kind, and the officers and men drew one-half bushel of corn as forage during the whole campaign.

CAPT. CHAMPION S. MADING'S COMPANY,

3d Regiment, 2d Brigade, of Illinois Mounted Volunteers, called into the service of the United States, on the requisition of Gen. Atkinson, by the Governor's proclamation, dated May 15, 1832. This company was organized and their officers commissioned May 5, 1832. Mustered out August 15, 1832, by order of Brig.-Gen. Atkinson.

Name and Rank.	Residence.	Enrolled	Remarks.
Captain.		1832	
Champion S. Mading	Edwards Co..	June 19	1 horse left, on forced march, during battle..
First Lieutenant.			
William Curtis......	"	"	Horse left, br'ke down; furl. Aug. 7 at P. Deesha
Second Lieutenant.			
Thomas Sanders	"	"	
Sergeants.			
James Hunt.........	"	"	
James Edmonson ...	"	"	Main spring U. S. gun broke................
James Ellison	"	"	
John Edmonson.....	"	"	
Corporals.			
Sam'l Edmonson, 2d.	"	"	12 days' rations, from 15th Aug. for 21 men....
Privates.			
Bogwood, David.....	"	"	
Cooper, John	"	"	Furloughed Aug. 7; 1 horse broke down......
Garland, Joseph.....	"	"	
Greathouse, David..	"	"	Furloughed Aug. 7; horse broke down........
Hill, Starlin........	"	"	Bayonet of U. S. gun lost.................
Mitchell, William....	"	"	
Mounts, Stephen	"	"	
Pixley, Lewis.......	"	"	
Russell, Robert......	"	"	Mainspring of U. S. gunlock broke...........
Rutherford, Josiah..	"	"	
Shelby, David	"	"	
Shelby, E...........	"	"	
Sames, L. B.........	"	"	
Shores, William	"	"	
Spring, Henry	"	"	Furloughed Aug. 7; 1 horse broke down......
Sterrit, John	"	"	
Waldrup, John	"	"	Furloughed Aug. 7, at battle-ground..........

Mustered out of service at Fort Dixon, under command of Capt. Jordan, of the 2d Regiment of 2d Brigade:

Name and Rank.	Residence.	Enrolled	Remarks.
Corporals.		1832	
Bell, James, 1st......	Edwards Co..	June 19	
Wilson, Elijah, 3d ...	"	"	
Bengaman, Wm., 4th.	"	"	

Name and Rank.	Residence.	Enrolled	Remarks.
Musician.		1832	
Drury, John.........	Edwards Co..	June 16	....
Privates.			
Bennit, James	"	"	....
Eppney, Gordon.....	"	"	....
Kelley, Milton.......	"	"	....
Lay, Josiah	"	"	....
Mading, Robt........	"	"	....
McKinney, Alfred ...	"	"	....
Moore, Harrison.....	"	"	....
Mays, Mathew.......	"	"	....
Mounts, Joseph......	"	"	....
Shelby, Jonathan ...	"	"	....
Thread, Robert......	"	"	....
Thread, James	"	"	....
Underwood, Alex....	"	"	....
Warren, William R..	"	"	....

No rations only as privates drawn by any commissioned officer in my company; only one-half bu. of corn drawn by each man during the time of service; only one-half gallon of spirits drawn by the company; not one pound of baggage hauled or packed for any commissioned officer in my company.

This company was ordered to rendezvous at Hennepin June 10, and arrived the 11th, and was mustered into service the 19th.

Capt. John Haynes' Company

Of the 3d Regiment, 2d Brigade, Mounted Volunteers of Illinois, called into the service of the United States by the Governor's proclamation, dated May 15, 1832. Mustered out of service August 15, 1832.

Name and Rank.	Residence.	Enrolled	Remarks.
Captain.		1832.	
John Haynes.........	White Co.....	June 19	....
First Lieutenant.			
Thomas Fields.......	"	"	....
Second Lieutenant.			
Reuben Emerson....	"	"	Sup. disch. under Capt. Jordan; halter lost..
Sergeants.			
Martin Johnson.....	"	"	Sup. disch. under Capt. Jordan; halter lost..
Pliny H. Gawdy......	"	"	Bucket, 1 pan and tin cup lost............
John Robinson.......	"	"	Saddle and equipage lost.................
Robert Lowry........	"	"	....
Corporals.			
John Penyman......	"	"	Sup. disch. under Capt. Jordan; horse, saddle
John Heine..........	"	"	Sick........................(and bridle lost.
Leand'r W. McKnight	"	"	Sup. disch. under Capt. Jordon; horse, &c., lost
James Fields........	"	"	....
Privates.			
Berry, Edward......	"	"	Sup. disch. under Capt. Jordan; halter lost..
Barnet, Harvey.....	"	"	Furloughed on Aug. 7, 1832...............
Fields, William.....	"	"	Bayonet lost.............................
Gott, Anthony......	"	"	....
Hunter, Philip P....	"	"	....
Hart, James W......	"	"	....
Hood, Henry........	"	"	Halter lost.............................
Johnson, Arthur L..	"	"	Sup. disch. under Capt. Jordan; halter lost..
Land, John..........	"	"	....
Martin, Asa.........	"	"	Furloughed on Aug. 7, 1832..............
Moody, John........	"	"	Supposed discharged under Capt. Jordan....
Moore, William.....	"	"	Furloughed on Aug. 7, 1832; halter lost....
McCan, Bartholom'w	"	"	....

SECOND BRIGADE.   43

Name and Rank.	Residence.	Enrolled	Remarks.
		1832	
McClarney, Robert..	White Co..	June 19	Sup. disch. under Capt. Jordan; halter lost..
Nation, John........	"	......	"	
Nation, Anderson...	"	......	"	Sup. disch. under Capt. Jordan; halter lost..
Nation, Thomas.....	"	......	"	
Nucum, Joseph......	"	......|	"	" " horse lost...
Odd, John S.........	"	......	"	
Orr, James..........	"	......	"	
Parker, Joseph M...	"	......	"	
Parker, George C...	"	......	"	Bayonet lost........
Peacock, John.......	"	......	"	
Porter, James.......	"	......	"	
Porter, William.....	"	......	"	
Patterson, Robert...	"	......	"	
Renshaw, Ebenezer.	"	......	"	Sup. disch. under Capt. Jordan; halter lost..
Teachner, Chad. R..	"	......	"	
Upton, John.........	"	......	"	Furloughed Aug. 7, 1832; halter lost.........
Wrenwick, James...	"	......|	"	Horse and halter lost........................
Young, Ninian......	"	......	"	Supposed discharged under Capt. Jordan....

This company was organized in the county of White on May 12, 1832, and was mustered into the service of the United States on June 19, 1832.

Capt. William Thomas' Company

Of the 3d Regiment, 2d Brigade of Mounted Volunteers of Illinois, called into the service of the United States by the Governor's proclamation, dated May 15, 1832; mustered out on August 15, 1832.

Name and Rank.	Residence.	Enrolled	Remarks.
Captain.		1832.	
William Thomas....	White Co...	June 19	....
First Lieutenant.			
Henry Horn.........	"	"	
Second Lieutenant.			
Joel Rice.............	"	"	
Sergeants.			
Thomas Culbreth...	"	"	
John M. Wilson.....	"	"	Supposed discharged under Capt. Jordan....
Peter Miller.........	"	"	Furloughed Aug. 6, 1832; horse, etc., lost....
Enoch B. Hargrave.	"	"	Sup. disch. under Capt. Jordan; horse lost..
Corporals.			
Wesley Jameison...	"	"	
James D. Thomas...	"	" .	
William Null........	"	"	
Green Bowen........	"	"	
Musician.			
William Greer......	"	"	Furloughed Aug. 7 ....
Privates.			
Anderson, Bayles...	"	"	Furloughed Aug. 6, 1832 ....
Byrd, John..........	"	"	Supposed discharged under Capt. Jordan....
Bowin, William.....	"	"	Furloughed Aug. 6, 1832......................
Bowin, Joshua......	"	"	
Brown, Joseph......	"	"	
Clark, Benj.........	"	"	Supposed discharged under Capt. Jordan....
Chism, James.......	"	"	
Culbreth, Thomas,Jr	"	"	
Clyburn, James F...	"	"	Horse, etc., lost; sup. furl. under Capt. Jordan
Goodman, Joseph...	"	"	
Gardner, Thomas...	"	"	Supposed discharged under Capt. Jordan....
Goodwin, Miles.....	"	"	Sup. disch. under Capt. Jordan; horse lost...
Harman, Daniel.....	"	"	
Hargrave, Samuel..	"	"	Horse and equipage lost......................
Hogue, Lewis D....	"	"	
Harman, John......	"	"	

Name and Rank.	Residence.	Enrolled	Remarks.
		1832.	
Jamison, John D. B.	White Co	June 19	
Johnson, William	"	"	Saddle lost.
Mears, James	"	"	
Mead, Alexander	"	"	Furloughed June 20, 1832; horse, etc., lost
Mears, Mark	"	"	Left sick at Fort Wilbourn June 20, 1832
Miller, William	"	"	Furloughed Aug. 7, 1832.
Russel, Hiram A.	"	"	
Staley, Ezekiel	"	"	Furloughed Aug. 7, 1832; horse, etc., lost
Thomas, John	"	"	
Vineyard, Joshua	"	"	
Woods, Thomas	"	"	
Wilson, William B.	"	"	Furloughed Aug. 7, 1832.

This company was organized in the county of White county May 12, 1832. Marched, according to the order of the Governor, on May 29, 1832. Mustered into the service on June 19, 1832.

Capt. Daniel Powell's Company

Of 3d Regiment, 2d Brigade of Illinois Mounted Volunteers, called into the service of the United States, on the requisition of Gen. Atkinson, by the Governor's proclamation dated May 15, 1832. Mustered out Aug. 15, 1832.

Name and Rank.	Residence.	Enrolled	Remarks.
Captain.		1832.	
Daniel Powell	White Co	July 19.	
First Lieutenant.			
Joshua Blackard	"	....	"	Furloughed at Coscannon by Gen. Atkinson.
Second Lieutenant.			
James Eubanks	"	....	"	Ordered to Dixon; supposed to be disch'd...
Sergeants.			
William Taylor	"	....	"	Horse lost June 28, 1832
Thos. M. Vineyard	"	....	"	Furl. from Prairie du Chien by Capt. Powell.
Thos. Joyner	"	....	"	Ordered to Dixon, and supposed discharged.
William Vickers	"	....	"	
Corporals.			
Alex. McKinsey	"	....	"	Furloughed August 6
John E. Ogburn	"	....	"	Ordered to Dixon; supposed discharged
Benjamin Rayney	"	....	"	Ord. to Dixon; sup. disch'd; horse, etc., lost.
William Miller	"	....	"	" " " "
Musician.			
Thomas Tary	"	....	"	Ordered to Dixon; supposed discharged
Privates.			
Askey, Elisha	"	....	"	Ordered to Dixon; supposed discharged
Briant, Henry	"	....	"	Furloughed Aug. 6
Barnett, James	"	....	"	
Burnett, David P.	"	....	"	
Butts, James W. G.	"	....	"	
Brill, John A	"	....	"	Furloughed Aug. 6.
Brill, Alfred L.	"	....	"	
Bowers, Singleton	"	....	"	
Bennett, Asa L.	"	....	"	Ordered to Dixon; supposed discharged
Briant, Daniel	"	....	"	Furloughed Aug. 6
Chapman, William	"	....	"	
Carson, John	"	....	"	Horse and equipage lost Aug. 11
Colbert, John	"	....	"	Ordered to Dixon; supposed discharged
Delap, John	"	....	"	
Daviss, Isaac	"	....	"	
Daviss, William	"	....	"	
Everlett, John	"	....	"	Ordered to Dixon; supposed discharged
Eubanks, James, Jr.	"	....	"	" " " "
Gross, William	"	....	"	
Garett, Peter	"	....	"	Horse lost Aug. 13, 1832
Haskins, John	"	....	"	Ordered to Dixon; supposed discharged
Holland, Hezekiah	"	....	"	

SECOND BRIGADE.

Name and Rank.	Residence.	Enrolled	Remarks.
Lewis, Jeremiah T.F.	White Co.	1832. July 19.	
Lasiter, Eneas A.	"	"	
Marion, Bartholo'ew	"	"	Left sick at Wilbourn; on furlough June 20.
McNutt, Sidney	"	"	Ordered to Dixon; supposed discharged.
Netson, James	"	"	
Pearce, Moses	"	"	
Pearce, James	"	"	
Porter, Robert W.	"	"	Ordered to Dixon; supposed discharged.
Pool, Thomas	"	"	
Rogers, Reuben	"	"	Ordered to Dixon; supposed discharged.
Trousdale, Abner L.	"	"	
Tucker, Wooddy	"	"	
Todd, Thomas	"	"	
Trout, Daniel	"	"	
Vickers, Thomas	"	"	Horse and equipage lost
Vaugh, William H.	"	"	Furloughed Aug. 6
Vickers, Eli	"	"	Horse lost Aug. 15; 1832.
Waters, Thomas	"	"	Furl. Aug. 6; horse and equipage lost Aug. 6.
Williss, James	"	"	
Williams, Alexander	"	"	
Williss, Alfred	"	"	

DETACHMENT OF CAPT. DAVID POWELL'S COMPANY

Of Illinois Mounted Volunteers, called into the service of the United States by the Governor of the State, by his order of May 15, 1832, from the date of its enrollment to August 2, 1832, when mustered out of service at Dixon's Ferry.

Name and Rank.	Residence.	Enrolled	Remarks.
Second Lieutenant.		1832	
James Eubanks	White Co.	June 16.	
Third Sergeant.			
Thomas Joiner	"	"	Horse lost in service
Corporals.			
John E. Ogburn	"	"	Horse lost in service
Benj. Ranney	"	"	
Wm. Miller	"	"	Horse lost in service
Privates.			
Askey, Elisha	"	"	
Bennett, Asa L.	"	"	
Coibert, John	"	"	Two blankets lost in service
Eubanks, James	"	"	
Everlet, John	"	"	
Gross, William	"	"	
Holland, Hezekiah	"	"	
Haskins, John	"	"	
Netson, James	"	"	Horse, saddle and bridle lost in service
McNutt, Sidney	"	"	Gun lost in service
Porter, Robt. W.	"	"	
Rogers, Rueben	"	"	Horse, saddle and bridle lost in service
Terry, Thomas	"	"	One rifle gun lost in service
Trousdale, A. L.	"	"	

SPY BATTALION.

Capt. John F. Richardson's Company,

Spy Battalion, 2d Brigade, Illinois Militia Mounted Volunteers, called into the service of the United States, on the requisition of Gen. Atkinson, by the Governor's proclamation dated May 15, 1832. Mustered out August 15, 1832, at Dixon's Ferry, Rock River, Illinois.

Name and Rank.	Residence.	Enrolled	Remarks.
Captain.		1832.	
John F. Richardson	Clark Co	June 5	
First Lieutenant.			
Woodford Dulaney			Furloughed and returned home Aug. 4, 1832.
Second Lieutenant.			
Justin Harlin			Ret. home, furl., Aug. 4, from Prairie du Chien
Sergeants.			
Jacob Dolson			Susp. from com'd June 29, at Prairie du Chien
John Wilson			Lost horse, saddle and bridle, $78, July 15.
Asher V. Burwell			Lost saddle and spancels, $18, August 1, 1832.
Robert Davidson			Horse gave out; left at Ft. Winnebago, July 15
Corporals.			
Christian Jeffers			
Nathan Hollenbach			
Richard Ross			
George Wilson			
Privates.			
Ashmore, Zeno A			
Biggs, Samuel M			Furn'd Martin L. Ashmore as subst. June 20.
Cooper, Franklin			Lost horse and saddle July 4; sup. disch.
Chenowith, Martin F			Mustered out of service in Capt. Notts' Co.
Cooper, Theopolus			
Davidson, Daniel			
Elliott, Aspano			Supposed to have been discharged
Hadden, Andrew			" " "
Hadden, Samuel			" " "
Hogue, Joseph			
Johnson, George			Supposed to be discharged
Kerr, John			
Locker, Conrad F			Lost his horse; supposed to be disch. July 22.
Markle, Joseph W			Supposed to have been discharged
Nott, Stephen			
Prevo, Samuel			Transferred to Capt. Notts' Co.
Prevo, Ira			
Shaw, Nineveh			Appointed Adjutant June 18, 1832.
Sharp, Cyrus			
Thomas, Martin			
Taylor, Robert			Deserted June 20; transferred from Co. roll.
Williams, James			
White, Gideon B			
White, Samuel			Lost his gun and blankets (priv. prop.) July 12
White, Luther			
White, Robert			
Wheeler, Tarleton			Lost his horse July 22; supposed to be disch.
Waters, John			Transferred to Capt. Notts' Co.
Yocum, Alexander			
Langham, Abel			Supposed to be discharged

Company was organized June 5, 1832, and marched from Fort Wilbourn June 9, 1832; mustered into the service of the United States June 19, 1832.

SECOND BRIGADE. 47

My company furnished themselves with eight days rations while on their march from Clark county to Fort Wilbourn. The officers, while in service, have drawn but one ration per day, and no forage has been furnished. My company rations have been drawn for the company to return home, viz: twelve days, up to and including the 30th day of Aug., 1832.

(Signed.)   JOHN F. RICHARDSON, Capt.

Capt. Abner Greer's Company,

Spy Battalion, of Illinois Mounted Volunteers, called into service of the United States, on the requisition of Gen. Atkinson, by the Governor's proclamation dated ——, 1832. Mustered out August 15, 1832.

Name and Rank.	Residence.	Enrolled	Remarks.
Captain.		1832.	
Abner Greer.........	Lawrence Co.	May 5...	Lost 1 pr. pistols worth $15—private property.
First Lieutenant.			
David D. Marney....	"	"	Lost horse, etc., val. $94; on furlough Aug. 2..
Second Lieutenant.			
Aaron Wells.........	"	"	" " " " " " "
Sergeants.			
Ebenezer Z. Ryan...	"	"	Furloughed at Fort Dodge, August 11........
William R. Jackman.	"	"	Lost horse and equipage valued at $70.50.....
Mason Jones.........	"	"	
Alex. H. Gilmore....	"	"	Absent on furlough ....
Corporals.			
James Gadd.........	"	"	Lost horse, etc., valued at $91.; furloughed...
Thomas B. Spencer..	"	"	Furloughed to return home..................
Jeremiah Cawthorn.	"	"	
Thomas J. England.	"	"	Lost horse and equipage.....................
Privates.			
Andrews, Silas......	"	"	Lost horse and equipage; furloughed.........
Blizard, Thomas....	"	"	" " " ....
Baird, James........	"	"	
Baird, Proctor B....	"	"	
Clubb, Eli..........	"	"	Furloughed Aug. 14, 1832...................
Cooper, John........	"	"	Lost horse; left on duty July 7.............
Dudley, Joshua.....	"	"	Furloughed Aug. 14, 1832...................
Dickerson, George...	"	"	Detached on duty July 19...................
Evans, William......	"	"	Lost horse Aug. 7; furloughed...............
England, David.....	"	"	
Fyte, Moses.........	"	"	Furloughed Aug. 14.........................
Fyffe, Edward P....	"	"	Left sick July 9............................
Fish, Josiah........	"	"	
Galaspie, William...	"	"	
Gibbons, Harvey....	"	"	
Jonady, Joseph......	"	"	
Jackman, Bazel.....	"	"	
Johnston, Abner....	"	"	Lost horse................................
Johnston, Robert...	"	"	Furloughed Aug. 14........................
Kirkling, Williamson	"	"	Detached June 20..........................
Kellams, Gideon....	"	"	Left on duty July 19.......................
Lawler, William.....	"	"	Furloughed Aug. 12........................
Lackey, John O.....	"	"	Lost horse; left on duty July 19............
Lackey, Thomas....	"	"	Left on duty July 19.......................
Neil, James.........	"	"	Left sick July 19..........................
Perkins, Thomas....	"	"	Furloughed August 14.....................
Pumphrey, Laonie..	"	"	Left sick July 19..........................
Pollard, Edwin.....	"	"	
Rawlings, Nathan...	"	"	Furloughed Aug. 14........................
Richards, Newton ..	"	"	
Small, Thomas H...	"	"	
Seeds, William......	"	"	Lost horse and equipage....................
Selby, Josiah........	"	"	Detailed on duty June 24..................
Williams, John......	"	"	Discharged July 19........................
Young, Jacob.......	"	"	Lost horse and equipage....................
Young, Jonathan....	"	"	

Thomas Spencer, a private of this company, was mustered into the service of the United States as a private of the company, mounted, armed and equipped, on the 19th of June, 1832, at Ft. Wilbourn. He served through the campaign and left the company in charge of a disabled man (T. B. Spencer) on the 10th and 11th of August, four or five days before the company was mustered out of service, and his name was omitted from this muster roll by oversight. He should have been mustered out of service upon this roll, and is fully entitled to pay during the full term of the company. To the truth of which I hereby certify on honor.

          (Signed.) A. GREER,
 LAWRENCEVILLE, May 3, 1833.   Capt. com'd'g company.

 This company was organized and enrolled on May 5, 1832, and took up line of march for Ft. Wilbourn on June 2, and was mustered into the service of the United States June 19, 1832.

CAPT. JOHN MCCANN'S COMPANY

Of Spy Battalion, 2d Brigade, Illinois Mounted Volunteers, called into the service of the United States on the requisition of Gen. Atkinson, by the Governor's proclamation, dated 1832. Mustered out of the service of the United States Aug. 15, 1832.

Name and Rank.	Residence.	Enrolled	Remarks.
Captain.		1832.	
John McCann	White Co	May 12	
First Lieutenant.			
Samuel Slocumb			Furloughed at Prairie du Chien Aug. 7, 1832
Second Lieutenant.			
Walter Burress			Sword, belonging to U. S., lost
Sergeants.			
William Garrison			
Solomon Garrison			
Noah Staley			Furloughed at Prairie du Chein; horse lost
James Keneda			Lost his horse and equipage
Corporals.			
Levi Wells			
William Stephens			
William Daniels			
Henry McCann			
Privates.			
Berry, George			Supposed to be discharged at Dixon's
Bailey, Alfred			Lost his horse and equipage
Britain, Joseph M			
Blackledge, John			Sick
Blackwell, James C			Supposed to be discharged at Dixon's
Cann, James			
Council, Willis			
Campbell, John			Lost his horse
Crowder, John			Furloughed at Prairie du Chien Aug. 7, 1832
Coonts, Thomas			
Edwards, Ambrose			
Evans, Jonathan			
Farley, Martin			Lost his saddle, bridle, blanket and halter
Farley, John			Supposed to be discharged at Dixon's Ferry
George, John			
George, Francis			Supposed to be discharged at Wilbourn
Goodman, James			Furloughed at Prairie du Chien Aug. 7, 1832
Hood, Allen			Supposed to be discharged at Dixon's
Hood, Anderson			
Hilyard, William			
Holderly, Dempsey			Lost his horse and equipage
Heasty, Daniel			Lost his horse
Hust, John			Lost his horse and equipage
Hamilton, Wm. S.			Supposed to be discharged at Wilbourn
Lindsey, Thomas J			
Lowe, Thomas			
McMullin, Wilkerson			
Nevett, Wm. G			Horse and equipage lost
Neslar, James			Supposed to be discharged at Dixon's
Parker, Wilson			
Robinson, Michael			Furloughed at Prairie du Chien Aug. 7, 1832
Robinson, Nich'l's A.			
Rippatoo, Burress			
Robinson, Aaron			
Stone, Thomas W	White Co		Supposed to be discharged at Dixon's Ferry
Smith, Slade			
Staley, George			Furloughed at Prairie du Chien August 7, 1832
Sutler, Rodolphus M.			Lost his horse and equipage

Name and Rank.	Residence.	Enrolled	Remarks.
		1832.	
Smith, Silas			Lost his horse and equipage
Wilson, Christopher			
Williams, Hardy			Supposed to be discharged at Dixon's

John C. Slocumb, of White county, volunteered, armed and equipped himself, and marched with the company from Carmi, took sick and was left at Fairfield, Wayne county. I am credibly informed, and believe, that said Slocumb afterwards reported himself for duty at Fort Wilbourn, and served there and as Wagon Guard between Fort Wilbourn and Dixon's Ferry, when he was discharged early in August and returned home.

(Signed.)   WM. McHENRY,
Major Spy Battalion.

This company enrolled under command of Wm. McHenry, Captain, May 12, 1832, and was mustered into the service of the United States June 19, 1832. John McCann was elected Captain in place of Wm. McHenry, promoted on June 18, 1832, and has commanded since.

DETACHMENTS.

A Detachment

Of Illinois Mounted Volunteers, under the command of Isaac Parmenter, Adjt. 2d Regiment, 2d Brigade, from the day of its enrollment to August 2, 1832, when mustered out of service, at Dixon's Ferry, Illinois.

Name and Rank.	Residence.	Enrolled	Remarks.
Adjutant.		1832.	
Isaac Parmeter	Wabash Co...	June 16.	Adjutant 2d Regiment, 2d Brigade
First Lieutenant.			
Samuel Fisher	"	....	"
Sergeants.			
Mathew Leatherland	"	....	"
John A. Dodds	"	....	"	Lost his horse, etc., June 17, at Ft. Wilbourn.
Corporals.			
Solomon Frair	"	....	"
John Golden	"	....	"
Ira Keen	"	....	"
Westley Wood	"	....	"
Privates.			
Buchanon, Jos. O	"	....	"
Buchanon, Henry K.	"	....	"
Besley, James	"	....	"
Bigley, William	"	....	"
Dodds, Joseph M.	"	....	"
Goddy, John	"	....	"
Garner, James	"	....	"	Lost horse, etc., July 12, at Ft. Winnebago
Golden, William	"	....	"
Hoyt, Jonathan S	"	....	"
McMullen, James	"	....	"
Miller, Barton S	"	....	"
Ochletree, John	"	....	"
Reel, Henry R	"	....	"	Lost horse, etc., July 21, at Rock River.
Smith, John O	"	....	"
Turner, Abner	"	....	"	Lost horse, etc., June 17, at Ft. Wilbourn.
Utter, John	"	....	"
Vanderhoof, Philip	"	....	"
Wear, Thomas	"	....	"
Wear, Harvey	"	....	"

Capt. Hiram Roundtree's Company, 2d Regiment.

Third Sergeant.		1832.	
Samuel Jackson	Montg'm'y Co.	June 16	
Private.			
Levi Booger		"	Lost horse, on June 25, at Dixon's Ferry

Capt. Hiram Kinade's Company, 2d Regiment.

		1832.	
Richard Rattan	Greene Co...	June 17	Lost horse in service June 25, Dixon's Ferry.
Daniel Rattan			
John C. Jordan			

Capt. Mayo's Company, 1st Regiment, 2d Brigade.

		1832.	
Abraham Sumter	Edgar Co	June 16.	

Capt. Earl Peirce's Company, 2d Regiment.

Name and Rank.	Residence.	Enrolled	Remarks.
		1832.	
Brawdy, John C	Edgar Co	June 16	Lost horse in service June 25, Dixon's Ferry.
Clark, William	"	"	
Harris, Abijah	"	"	
McCarty, Nathan	"	"	Lost horse in service, June 25, Dixon's Ferry.
Shire, Jonathan	"	"	

Capt. Bennett Howlin's Company, 4th Regiment, 3d Brigade.

Name and Rank.	Residence.	Enrolled	Remarks.
		1832.	
Jacob Gibson	Macoupin Co.	June 17	

Capt. Solomon Hunter's Company, 3d Regiment, 2d Brigade.

Name and Rank.	Residence.	Enrolled	Remarks.
		1832	
Everly, Nimrod	Edwards Co	June 16.	
Morris, Miles	"	"	Lost saddle in service July 4, at Rock River.
Morris, George	"	"	
Vincin, Josiah	"	"	

Capt. John F. Richardson's Company, Spy Battalion, 2d Brigade.

Name and Rank.	Residence.	Enrolled	Remarks.
		1832.	
Ashmore, Martin L		June 16	Lost mare in service June 17, Ft. Wilbourn..
Ashmore, Zeno A		"	
Cooper, Franklin		"	Lost horse in service July 3, near Rock River
Johnson, George		"	" mare " July 6, on Rock River..

Capt. Isaac Sandford's Company, 1st Regiment, 2d Brigade.

Name and Rank.	Residence.	Enrolled	Remarks.
		1832.	
Davis, Abraham	Edgar Co		

CAPT. HIGHSMITH'S DETACHMENT

Of Illinois Mounted Volunteers, called into the service of the United States by the Governor of the State of Illinois, by his order of May 15, 1832, from the date of its enrollment to Aug. 2, 1832, when mustered out of service at Dixon's Ferry, Ill.

Name and Rank.	Residence.	Enrolled	Remarks.
Captain.		1832.	
Wm. Highsmith	Crawford Co..	June 16	Horse and saddle lost in service
First Lieutenant.			
Samuel V. Allison	"	"	
Second Lieutenant.			
John H. McMickle	"	"	Horse lost. July 15, 1832
Sergeants.			
Thomas Fuller, 2d	"	"	Horse and saddle lost
William McCoy, 3d	"	"	Saddle lost
Corporals.			
Nathan Highsmith, 1.	"	"	
Martin Fuller, 2d	"	"	
John Lagon, 4th	"	"	

Name and Rank.	Residence.	Enrolled	Remarks.
Privates.		1832.	
Allison, John	Crawford Co.	June 16	
Allison, Samuel H	"	"	
Brimbery, John	"	"	
Carter, Benjamin	"	"	Horse and saddle lost
Easton, Thomas	"	"	
Garrison, Peter	"	"	
Johnston, John	"	"	
Kinney, George W.	"	"	
Lewis, James	"	"	Horse and saddle lost
Montgomery, And'w.	"	"	
Martin, Isaac	"	"	
Parker, John, Jr	"	"	Horse and saddle lost
Parker, Thomas N	"	"	
Phelps, Amos	"	"	
Stockwell, Thomas	"	"	
Reed, William	"	"	Horse, saddle and gun lost
Weger, James	"	"	Saddle lost

Capt. A. M. Houston's Company, 2d Regt., 2d Brigade.

Name and Rank.	Residence.	Enrolled	Remarks.
Corporals.		1832.	
Cornelius Doherty	Crawford Co.	June 16	
Joseph Jones	"	"	
Privates.			
Baugher, George	"	"	
Donden, George R	"	"	
Hacket, Joseph	"	"	
Hawkins, Wm.	"	"	
McCoy, John	"	"	
Pearson, Joseph	"	"	
Pearson, Edward	"	"	Horse and saddle lost
Pearson, William	"	"	
Phelps, Zilman	"	"	Horse lost
Vanderinder, John	"	"	

Capt. John Barns' Company, 2d Regt., 2d Brigade.

Name and Rank.	Residence.	Enrolled	Remarks.
Captain.		1832.	
John Barns	Lawrence Co.	June 16	Horse died in service July 4, 1832
First Lieutenant.			
Elijah Mays	"	"	Absent on furlough
Sergeants.			
James Nabb	"	"	Absent on furlough
Samuel Mundle	"	"	
Wm. Mase	"	"	
Corporals.			
A. S. Badollett	"	"	
Arthur Chenoweth	"	"	Absent on furlough
Joseph F. Darr	"	"	
Privates.			
Barns, Silas	"	"	
Bush, John	"	"	
Hunter, John T	"	"	Promoted to Quartermaster July 10, 1832
Lewis, Stephen S	"	"	
Moore, Tilford	"	"	
Mullins, John R	"	"	Horse and saddle lost
Organ, Daniel A	"	"	
Pea, Henry	"	"	
Pea, Samuel	"	"	
Pulls, John J	"	"	Absent on furlough
Rawlings, Frederick	"	"	Horse lost in service, and saddle
Ruark, John W	"	"	
Ruark, Wm. F	"	"	
Stewart, Joseph	"	"	Horse and saddle lost
Strother, Pendleton	"	"	Absent on furlough
Thompson, James	"	"	Wounded; left at Hosp., at Dixon's, Aug. 2, '32
Westfall, Isaac	"	"	

SECOND BRIGADE.

Capt. Abner Grear's Company, Spy Battalion, 2d Brigade.

Name and Rank.	Residence.	Enrolled	Remarks.
Privates.		1832.	
Andrews, Silas	Lawrence Co.	June 16.	
Cooper, John M	"	"	Left as attendant for Thompson; horse left.
Dickerson, George	"	"	
Fyffe, Edward P	"	"	
Kellams, Gideon	"	"	
Lackey, John O	"	"	
Lackey, Thomas	"	"	
Neil, James	"	"	
Pumphrey, Loami	"	"	
Selvy, Joseph			

THIRD BRIGADE.

FIRST REGIMENT.

CAPT. DAVID SMITH'S COMPANY

Of Mounted Volunteers, called and mustered into the service of the United States by order of the Commander-in-Chief of the Militia of the State of Illinois, attached to the 1st Regiment, 3d Brigade, under the command of Brig.-Gen. Henry Atkinson, from June 1, 1832, to August 1, 1832, when mustered out of service. Distant from Atlas, Madison county, 300 miles.

Name and Rank.	Residence.	Enrolled	Remarks.
Captain. David Smith	Madison Co.	1832. June 1.	
First Lieutenant. John Lee	" "	"	On furlough
Second Lieutenant. John Umphrey	" "	"	
Sergeants. S. I. Kendall	" "	"	
James Sterett	" "	"	
S. B. Gillhour	" "	"	
W. B. Crowder	" "	"	
Corporals. C. Subastian	" "	"	
S. N. P. Elliott	" "	"	
D. H. Fouquerer	" "	"	
John Walker	" "	"	
Privates. Brazil, S.	" "	"	
Brown, U.	" "	"	
Bangs, O.	Morgan Co.	"	Hospital Steward at Ottawa
Dunlap, R. M. C.	Madison Co.	"	
Drennan, C.	" "	"	
Drennan, I.	" "	"	
Dilliplain, I. P.	" "	"	
Eakin, T.	" "	"	
Harrison, W.	" "	"	
Hart, A.	" "	"	
Haynes, John	" "	"	
Hewes, I.	" "	"	
Kistler, W.	" "	"	
Kellogg, E.	LaSalle Co.	June 29.	
Loman, T.	Madison Co.	" 1.	
Makun, I.	" "	July 26.	
Nowland, John	" "	"	
Peter, C.	" "	"	
Pembroke, D.	" "	"	
Rogers, D. B.	" "	"	
Scott, John	" "	"	
Summers, H. S.	" "	"	
Slayton, J. M.	" "	"	

THIRD BRIGADE. 55

Name and Rank.	Residence.	Enrolled	Remarks.
		1832	
Shaw, I. E............	LaSalle Co...	June 29	....
Sprague, H. A.......	" "	" "	Sick at Ottawa.......................
Sprague, G...........	" "	" "	....
Wood, S..............	Madison Co..	" 1	....
Wheeler, E...........	" "	" 18	....
Lowell, N............	" "	" 1	....

Capt. William Gillham's Company

Of Mounted Volunteers, called and mustered into the service of the United States, by order of the Commander-in-Chief of the Militia of the State of Illinois, attached to the 1st Regiment of the 3d Brigade, under the command of Brigadier-General James D. Henry, from April 30, 1832. Mustered out at Fort Wilbourn Aug. 1, 1832.

Name and Rank.	Residence.	Enrolled	Remarks.
Captain.		1832.	
William Gillham....	Morgan Co...	April 30	....
First Lieutenant.			
Robert H. McDow...	" "	" "	On furlough...........................
Second Lieutenant.			
James Etheal........	" "	" "	....
Sergeants.			
Daniel Clotfelter....	" "	" "	....
William Leib........	" "	" "	....
John Sergeant.......	" "	" "	On furlough...........................
Aquilla Clarkson....	" "	" "	....
Corporals.			
Zadoc Riggs.........	" "	" "	....
Samuel Vanslyke...	" "	" "	....
James Morris........	" "	" "	....
Isaac Graton........	" "	" "	On furlough...........................
Privates.			
Arnett, John........	" "	" "	....
Apple, John.........	" "	" "	....
Avery, Joel.........	" "	" "	....
Baker, John.........	" "	" "	....
Bell, Alexander.....	" "	" "	Appointed Paymaster June 19, 1832......
Clarkson, Kinza.....	" "	" "	....
Clanton, Isaac......	" "	" "	....
Campbell, William..	" "	" "	....
Clarkson, Constant'e	" "	" "	On furlough...........................
Carter, Vincin......	" "	" "	....
Duvall, Nicholas....	" "	" "	....
Garmon, George....	" "	" "	....
Gillham, James.....	" "	" "	Elected Lieut.-Col. June 19, 1832.
House, H. W........	" "	" "	On furlough...........................
Halloway, James....	" "	" "	....
King, John..........	" "	" "	....
Kemp, Emanuel.....	" "	" "	....
Kemp, Murphy......	" "	" "	....
Lemon, H. H........	" "	" "	....
Murphy, Seth C.....	" "	" "	....
Mathers, William...	" "	" "	....
McCullom, Robert..	" "	" "	....
McConnel, John....	" "	" "	....
Masters, Squire D...	" "	" "	....
Nichols, Clark......	" "	" "	On furlough...........................
Northcutt, Archabel	" "	" "	....
Ovear, William.....	" "	" "	....
Olney, Washington.	" "	" "	Taken as wagoner; absent June 19, 1832...
Piper, James........	" "	" "	....
Riggs, Henry L......	" "	" "	....
Ragfield, James.....	" "	" "	On furlough...........................
Shelton, Seebert C..	" "	" "	....
Scott, Levi.........	" "	" "	....
Smith, William R...	" "	" "	....

Name and Rank.	Residence.	Enrolled	Remarks.
		1832.	
Smith, George	Morgan Co...	April 30	
Simmons, Mastin G.	"	"	
Whitley, Alexander.	"	"	
Wilkison, Alexander	"	"	
Willson, Clinton	"	"	

Capt. William Gorden's Company

Of Mounted Volunteers of Illinois Militia, ordered into the service of the United States by the Governor of the State, on the requisition of Gen. Atkinson, of U. S. Army. Attached to 1st Regiment, 3d Brigade, in the year 1832. Mustered out of service July 29, 1832, 212 miles from place of enrollment. Mustered into service June 2, 1832.

Name and Rank.	Residence.	Enrolled	Remarks.
Captain,		1832.	
William Gorden		April 30	
First Lieutenant,			
John Pickering		"	On furlough since July 19, 1832
Second Lieutenant.			
Thomas Askens		"	
Sergeants.			
Robert Dinsmore		"	
William York		"	On furlough since July 10, 1832
Sylvester Moss		"	
Benjamin Allen		"	
Corporals.			
Benjamin Murphy		"	On furlough since July 12, 1832
Loyd Aday		"	
Enoch Bramson		"	
John Dinsmore		"	
Privates.			
Allen, James G		"	
Black, Thomas G		"	
Boothby, Daniel		"	
Branson, Miram K		"	Appointed Asst. Surgeon June 19, 1832
Coonrod, Woolery		"	On furlough since July 10, 1832
Davis, Hugh		"	
Drummond, Patter'n		"	
Dinsmore, Mathew		"	
Garret, Hiram		"	
Hardwick, Rice		"	On furlough since July 18, 1832
Jones, Daniel R.		"	" " 19, 1832
Jones, William		"	
Johnson, James		"	
Kellogg, Orvill E.		"	On furlough since July 10, 1832
Keller, Joseph		"	
McGovern, Edward		"	Sent on express to Gen. Atkinson July 20, '32; [M. O. Aug. 2, '32.
Murphy, Dudley R.		"	
McDowell, Nelson		"	
Mills, William N.		"	
McCombs, Elijah		"	
Ogg, James		"	On furlough since July 19, 1832
Powell, Farington		"	
Powell, Henry		"	
Smith, Drury		"	
Strade, Malen		"	
Scott, Benjamin		"	
Slotten, Joseph		"	On furlough since July 26, 1832
Thomas, Manley		"	
Turner, William		"	
Williams, Elza		"	[M. O. Aug. 2, '32.
Weeks, Washington		"	Sent on express to Gen. Atkinson, July 20, '32.
Wood, Elisha K		"	Appointed Surgeon June 18, 1832

Capt. George F. Bristow's Company

Of Mounted Volunteers, called and mustered into the service of the United States, by order of the Commander-in-Chief of the Militia of the State of Illinois, attached to the 1st Regiment under the command of Col. Samuel T. Matthews, of the 3d Brigade, commanded by Brig. Gen. James D. Henry, from May 21, 1832, for and during the term of 90 days from said date. Mustered out at Fort Wilbourn Aug. 1, 1832.

Name and Rank.	Residence.	Enrolled	Remarks.
Captain.		1832	
George T. Bristow..	Morgan Co...	May 21	
First Lieutenant.			
Stephen Henderson.	" "	"	On furlough
Second Lieutenant.			
Walter Ellis..........	" "	"	
Sergeants.			
Allen Mattock......	" "	"	
George Thompson..	" "	"	
James Y. Logston...	" "	"	
Asa L. Lane..........	" "	"	
Privates.	Ottawa.		
Brown, James.......	LaSalle Co..	July 1..	
Combs, John.........	Morgan Co...	May 21	
Constant, Archibald			
Clemens, Willey L..	" "	"	
Carter, George......	" "	"	Deserted June 30, 1832.
Foster, Geo. W......	" "	"	
Henry, Thomas......	" "	"	
Hopper, William S..	" "	"	
Henderson, Nathan'l	" "	"	On furlough
Hull, William........	Ottawa.	"	
Hicks, Henry W.....	LaSalle Co..	July 1..	
Meeks, Allen.........	Morgan Co...	May 21	
Marshall, John......	" "	"	
Mackey, Daniel......	" "	"	
Moss, Isaac...........	" "	"	
Ream, Michael......	" "	"	
Thompson, Oswell .	" "	"	
Turney, Russell.....	" "	"	
Wilcox, John.........	LaSalle Co..	July 1..	
Warren, Ezekiel.....	" "	"	

Capt. S. T. Matthews',
afterwards
Capt. J. T. Arnett's Company

Of Mounted Volunteers, now under the command of 1st Lieut. D. B. McConnell, called and mustered into the service of the United States by order of the Commander-in-Chief of the Militia of the State of Illinois, belonging to the 1st Regiment, 3d Brigade. Mustered out August 1, 1832.

Name and Rank.	Residence.	Enrolled	Remarks.
Captain.		1832.	
S. T. Matthews......	Morgan Co..	May 5.	Promoted to Colonel June 19, 1832
First Lieutenant.			
N. H. Johnson.......	" "	"	Appointed to Staff of Brigade June 20
Second Lieutenant.			
D. B. McConnell.....	" "	"	Promoted to 1st Lieut. June 19, 1832
Sergeants.			
Josiah Gorham......	" "	"	
John Moss............	" "	"	Furloughed July 24, 1832
Sam'l P. Devone.....	" "	"	
Moses R. Bennett ...	" "	"	Furloughed July 3, 1832

Name and Rank.	Residence.	Enrolled	Remarks.
Corporals.		1832.	
John Sparks	Morgan Co.	May 5.	Furloughed July 18, 1832
Henry Moss	"	"	" " 24, 1832
L. B. Tankersby	"	"	
John Rusk	"	"	Furloughed July 18, 1832
Privates.			
Antle, Anderson	"	"	
Arnett, James	"	"	Promoted to Capt. June 19; resigned July 25.
Buchanan, Benj.	"	"	
Buchanan, Reuben	"	"	
Blair, James H.	"	"	
Cassell, James	"	"	
Crane, Harvey	"	"	
Courtney, Robert C.	"	"	
Clayton, Madison	"	"	
Colton, John L.	"	"	
Durant, Samuel	"	"	
Devore, James H.	"	"	
Duncan, Wm.	"	"	
Deads, Phillip	"	"	
Deal, Isaac	"	"	Detailed for use of Brigade June 24, 1832.
Evans, James	"	"	Promoted to Major June 19, 1832.
Edwards, John	"	"	
Farris, Jonathan	"	"	
Graves, James H.	"	"	Sick and discharged June 14, 1832.
Gilmore, John	"	"	
Goodpaster, Madis'n	"	"	
Hawkins, Wm. B.	"	"	
Howard, Alanson	"	"	
Hurst, John	"	"	Furloughed July 18, 1832
Hobbs, Silas	"	"	
Hunter, Henry	"	"	
Henry, John	"	"	
Hook, Cornelius	"	"	Appointed to Staff of Brigade June 14.
Holland, Berry	"	"	
Ingles, Darius	"	"	
Johnson, John	"	"	
Jarrod, Moses	"	"	
Jordan, Wm. L.	"	"	
Johnson, Abraham	"	"	
Lycock, Thomas	"	"	
Lamples, Jacob	"	"	Lost his horse
Lash, James	"	"	
Mounts, Matthias	"	"	Promoted to 2d Lieut. June 19, 1832.
Million, Elijah F.	"	"	
McConnel, Murray	"	"	Appointed to Staff of Brigade June 19, 1832.
Pitner, Alex	"	"	
Pitner, Montgomery	"	"	
Roberts, Milton B.	"	"	Appointed to Staff June 19.
Richards, John	"	"	
Sweet, Dan'l	"	"	
Slocumb, John C.	"	July 14.	
Tolley, James	"	May 5.	Furloughed July 18, 1832
Turner, Jonathan	"	"	
Williams, David	"	"	Permitted to leave the company June 22, sick

Capt. Walter Butler's Company

Of Illinois Mounted Volunteers, in the service of the United States, under Brig.-Gen. H. Atkinson. Mustered out of service August 1, 1832.

Name and Rank.	Residence.	Enrolled	Remarks.
Captain.		1832.	
Walter Butler	Morgan Co.	June 4	
First Lieutenant.			
Thomas P. Ross	"	"	
Second Lieutenant.			
Fleming C. Maupin	"	"	

THIRD BRIGADE.

Name and Rank.	Residence.	Enrolled	Remarks.
Sergeants.		1832.	
Samuel Givens	Morgan Co.	June 4.	
Achilles Deatherage	"	"	
David Hart	"	"	
David Mackey	"	"	
Corporals.			
Nathan Hart	"	"	Appointed Q. M. Sergeant June 19, 1832
Henderson Vickens	"	"	
John L. Heffington	"	"	
William T. Nall	"	"	
Privates.			
Auston, Eli	"	"	Substitute for And. Wyatt
Beason, Henry	"	"	
Brown, John	"	"	Substitute for Eli Auston
Brown, Joseph	"	"	Furloughed June 24, during term of service
Clayton, Jesse	"	"	Substitute for John Sappington
Dougherty, John	"	"	
Davidson, David	"	"	
Fanning, George	"	"	
Fanning, Washing'n	"	"	
Fanning, Abraham	"	"	
Groves, James	"	"	
Gilleland, Thomas	"	"	
Haynes, Bluford	"	"	
Hart, Anderson	"	"	
Harris, Thomas I.	"	"	
Hart, Charles	"	"	Furloughed June 24, during term of service
Kirby, James	"	"	
Keplinger, Isaac	"	"	
Murphy, Nimrod C.	"	"	
Minor, Samuel C.	"	"	Furloughed June 24, during term of service
Nall, John	"	"	
Norvell, Spencer	"	"	
Patterson, William	"	"	Substitute for Hiram Patterson
Porter, Ephriam	"	"	" Jas. Hutcherson
Pryon, James	"	"	
Ray, Robert	"	"	Furloughed on July 10, 1832, for 25 days
Riggs, Archibald	"	"	Substitute for John Love
Ross, John W	"	"	Elected 1st Corporal June 19; N. Hart prom.
Seamore, Edward	"	"	
Seamore, Richards'n	"	"	
Scott, James	"	"	
Stewart, Charles	"	"	
Talkington, William	"	"	
Wright, George	"	"	
Wiggs, Daniel	"	"	Substitute for John Still
Woods, John	"	"	
Weatherford, Wm	"	"	Appointed Adjutant June 19, 1832

SECOND REGIMENT

Capt. Hiram Roundtree's Company

Of 2d Regiment, 3d Brigade of Illinois Mounted Volunteers, called into the service of the United States on the requisition of Gen. Atkinson, by the Governor's proclamation dated May 15, 1832. This company was organized May 21, 1832, in Montgomery county, Illinois, Mustered out August 16, 1832.

Name and Rank.	Residence.	Enrolled	Remarks.
Captain.		1832.	
Hiram Roundtree...	Montg'm'y Co	June 20.	
First Lieutenant.			
John Kirkpatrick....	" "	" "	
Second Lieutenant.			
Thomas Philips.....	" "	" "	
Sergeants.			
Andrew K. Gray.....	" "	" "	
John Stone..........	" "	" "	
Samuel Jackson.....	" "	" "	Sent home sick from Korkonory July 9, 1832.
David B. Starr......	" "	" "	
Corporals.			
Spartan Grisham....	" "	" "	
Malaki Smith.......	" "	" "	
Thomas McAdams..	" "	" "	Permitted to return home another way
Thomas Edwards ...	" "	" "	
Privates.			
Aydlett, Clement C..	" "	" "	Discharged by order of Gen. Scott....
Brown, John........	" "	" "	Sent home sick from Korkonory, July 9, 1832.
Briggs, John.......	" "	" "	
Burke, Joseph......	" "	" "	
Berry, James M.....	" "	" "	
Booer, Levi W......	" "	" "	Discharged by Gen. Scott; horse lost; val. $60
Coffey, Cleaveland..	" "	" "	
Copeland, David....	" "	" "	
Carlew, John	" "	" "	
Cardwell, James	" "	" "	Sent home sick from Korkonory July 9, 1832.
Duncan, John	" "	" "	
Early, Thomas	" "	" "	
Evans, Thomas.....	" "	" "	
Forehand, Ammon..	" "	" "	
Griffith, William....	" "	" "	
Gray, Thomas......	" "	" "	Discharged at Helena July 28, 1832.
Gray, Alexander R..	" "	" "	
Hart, John	" "	" "	
Harkey, George.....	" "	" "	Sent home sick
Holmes, John M....	" "	" "	" " " " from Fort Wilbourn June 22.
Harkey, William	" "	" "	
Heady, Thomas W..	" "	" "	
Hughes, Thomas C..	" "	" "	Sent home by water; horse disabled; val. $60
Hannah, John	" "	" "	
Johnson, Alfred	" "	" "	
Jones, William	" "	" "	
Johnson, Jesse	" "	" "	
Johnson, Thomas...	" "	" "	
Lockerman, James..	" "	" "	
Long, John K.......	" "	" "	[march after enemy.
McCurry, John	" "	" "	Sent to Galena sick; horse, etc., lost on forced
McPhnill, Malcolm..	" "	" "	
McCullock, David T.	" "	" "	

THIRD BRIGADE.

Name and Rank.	Residence.	Enrolled	Remarks.
		1832.	
Mansfield, Horace	Montg'm'y Co	June 20	Discharged by Gen. Atkinson
McCullock, Axrin	"	"	
McCullock, Robert	"	"	
McWilliams, John M.	"	"	Permitted to go home by water
McDavid, William	"	"	
Paisley, Samuel	"	"	
Potter, Thomas	"	"	[march after enemy.
Potter, James	"	"	Sent to Galena sick; horse, etc., lost on forced
Rhodes, Jacob	"	"	Discharged by Gen. Scott
Rose, Willis	"	"	
Steel, Luke Sea	"	"	
Sturtevant, Thomas	"	"	Sent home June 22, as attendant on sick
Shirley, Zebedee	"	"	Permitted to go home before mustering out
Slater, John	"	"	Horse, etc., value $62, lost on forced march.
Tennis, William M.	"	"	
Wilson, James	"	"	
Williams, David M.	"	"	
Williams, William S.	"	"	
Wilson, Joseph W.	"	"	Sent home by water, sick
Wood, Thomas	"	"	" sick from Ft. Wilbourn June 22
Williford, Thomas	"	"	Sent to Galena sick
Young, William	"	"	

This company was organized in Montgomery county, Illinois, May 21, 1832. Ordered to march June 4, and actually marched June 9, and was mustered into the service of the U. S. at Fort Wilbourn, June 20, 1832.

CAPT. JAMES KINCAID'S COMPANY,

2d Regiment, 3d Brigade of Illinois Mounted Volunteers, called into the service of the United States, on the requisition of Gen. Atkinson, by the Governor's proclamation dated May 15, 1832. Mustered out August 16, 1832.

Name and Rank.	Residence.	Enrolled	Remarks.
		1832.	
Captain. James Kincaid	Carrollton. Greene Co.	June 19	Lost two horses on forced march
First Lieutenant. John Fry	"	"	
Second Lieutenant. Royal W. Pitts	"	"	Sick in quarters
Sergeants. John Link	"	"	
George Meldrum	"	"	
Henry Coonrod	"	"	
Christoph'r Dodgson	"	"	
Corporals. William McDorman	"	"	
Hugh Jackson	"	"	
John Coonrod	"	"	
Joseph M. Schuyler	"	"	Lost a horse
Privates. Biss, James	"	"	
Briggs, Thomas	"	"	Furloughed Aug. 12; lost a horse
Burton, Lemuel	"	"	
Coonrod, George	"	"	
Cook, Henry	"	"	
Cook, William	"	"	
Doughty, Felix	"	"	Lost a horse on forced march; sick in q'rt'rs.
Davis, Joshua	"	"	
Fry, Noah	"	"	
Finley, William	"	"	Furloughed August 2
Finley, Zuriah	"	"	
Green, Isaac B.	"	"	Lost a horse
Harrison, Fielding	"	"	Furloughed Aug. 2
Johnson, John	"	"	
Jordan, John C.	"	"	Discharged by order of Gen. Scott Aug. 2.

Name and Rank.	Residence.	Enrolled	Remarks.
Johnson, Robert	Carrollton. Greene Co.	1832 June 19	Discharged June 22; ill-health
Lewis, William	"	"	
Link, Mathias L.	"	"	Lost a horse
Linder, George	"	"	
Mongold, John	"	"	
Mellon, David	"	"	
Noris, James L.	"	"	Discharged June 22; ill-health
Rattan, Hiram	"	"	Absent with leave
Rattan, Larkin	"	"	Lost a horse
Rattan, Jarvis B.	"	"	
Rattan, Littleton	"	"	Furloughed Aug. 2
Rattan, Daniel	"	"	Disch. by Gen. Scott, Aug. 2; lost a horse
Rattan, Richard	"	"	
Sterling, Morse	"	"	
Stone, Asa	"	"	
Standifer, Isreal	"	"	
Waggoner, David	"	"	
Woodman, Austin	"	"	Furloughed Aug. 12
Whitesides, John B.	"	"	
Whitesides, Wm. H.	"	"	

This company, May 6, 1832, received orders to march June 3d. Marched June 6th. Arrived at Fort Wilbourn, the appointed place of rendezvous, June 14th, and was mustered into service June 19th. This company found its own rations in full from the 6th of June to the 16th of June. Since the 16th of June nearly all the small rations have been furnished by the company. No forage has ever been issued to this company. No officer of this company has ever drawn more rations than a private.

N. B.—By small rations, we mean candles, soap and all other articles furnished for soldiers, except flour and pork.

Capt. Gershom Patterson's Company

Of the 2d Regiment, 3d Brigade, of the Illinois Mounted Volunteers, called into the service of the United States, on the requisition of Gen. Atkinson, by the Governor's proclamation, dated May 15, 1832. This company was organized at the Rich Woodson, May 2, 1832. Mustered out Aug. 15, 1832, by order of Brig.-Gen. Atkinson.

Name and Rank.	Residence.	Enrolled	Remarks.
Captains.		1832.	
Alexander Smith	Greene Co	June 19.	Resigned July 15, 1832
Gershom Patterson	"	"	Promoted Captain July 16, 1832
First Lieutenant.			
Jacob Baccus	"	"	Horse and saddle lost Aug. 9, '32, forc'd march
Second Lieutenant.			
Samuel Bowman	"	"	Killed in battle Aug. 2, 1832
Sergeants.			
Jonathan Cooper	"	"	Detailed on extra duty for Qr.-Master
Calvin Piggs	"	"	
James Novin	"	"	Lost horse; on furlough
Alexander Moore	"	"	
Corporals.			
John Reddish	"	"	
Alexander Lyberly	"	"	
Edmund Medford	"	"	Saddle lost in action
Robert Irwin	"	"	
Privates.			
Bonner, Alexander	"	"	On furlough from July 20, 1832
Bowm, John	"	"	" " August 7, 1832
Chowning, Robert	"	"	
Chapman, Thos. H.	"	"	
Carlin, Thomas	"	"	Lost horse, saddle and bridle, forced march
Chisam, Alexander	"	"	
Clifford, Joseph	"	"	
Darnell, Isaac	"	"	Color bearer. Gun lost in battle
English, John N.	"	"	
McFaine, John	"	"	On furlough: lost horse, etc., forced march
Gufly, John	"	"	lost horse
Higgins, Phillonson	"	"	Lost horse, saddle and bridle, forced march
Hamilton, Bush. W.	"	"	

THIRD BRIGADE.

Name and Rank.	Residence.	Enrolled	Remarks.
		1832.	
Higgins, John	Greene Co.	June 19.	
McKinney, Joseph	"	"	On furlough from August 7, 1832.
Moore, Seabourn I.	"	"	
Means, James	"	"	
Means, John	"	"	
Mannon, David	"	"	
Rice, Solomon	"	"	
Rusk, David	"	"	On furlough from August 7, 1832.
Sears, Thomas	"	"	
Suttlemers, David	"	"	
Walden, Solomon	"	"	
Walden, John	"	"	

Resignation of Capt. Alexander Smith July 15, 1832. Samuel Bowman, 2d Lieut., fell in battle August 2, 1832. This company was organized May 2, 1832, and marched June 9, 1832, to Fort Wilbourn, and was mustered into service June 19, 1832. Gershom Patterson promoted to Captain July 16, 1832. Drawn eight days' rations for the purpose of taking the company to their respective homes. The company furnished their own provisions from the 9th to the 18th of June, 1832.

CAPT. AARON BANNON'S COMPANY

Of the 2d Regiment, 3d Brigade of Illinois Mounted Volunteers, called into the service of the United States, on the requisition of Gen. Atkinson, by the Governor's proclamation, dated May 15, 1832. This company organized, etc., in White Hall, Greene county, Illinois, June 5, 1832. Mustered out of service Aug. 16, 1832.

Name and Rank.	Residence.	Enrolled	Remarks.
Captain.		1832.	
Aaron Bannon	Greene Co.	June 19	
First Lieutenant.			
Harvey Jarboe	"	"	
Second Lieutenant.			
Job Collins	"	"	
Sergeants.			
James C. Campbell	"	"	
Absolom Kitchens	"	"	
Uriah Allen	"	"	
James Doddy	"	"	Discharged on account of inability July 15.
Corporals.			
Alexander W. Webb	"	"	Horse lost.
Hezekiah Crawsby	"	"	
Job Phillips	"	"	
John Jones	"	"	
Privates.			
Bishop, John	"	"	
Breeden, Peter	"	"	
Brantly, Josiah	"	"	
Banon, William	Macoupin Co.	"	On extra duty.
Conlee, Rheuben	Greene Co.	"	Ordered on special duty June 22.
Cartwright, Thomas	"	"	
Drummons, Benj.	"	"	
Evelin, Frederick	"	"	
Evans, Joseph	"	"	
Fisher, Samuel A.	"	"	Horse lost.
Ford, James	"	"	
Goss, Sherman	"	"	
Hart, James	"	"	Horse lost.
Hart, John F.	"	"	
Han, Henry	"	"	
Hunter, Jesse	"	"	
Morrison, Haman	"	"	Furloughed June 22 from Ft. Wilbourn, sick.
Magruder, Edmd. B.	"	"	
Manley, Gabriel	"	"	
McClanan, Jonatn. A.	"	"	
Pope, George	"	"	Horse lost.
Phillips, Edward	"	"	Furloughed June 22 from Ft. Wilbourn, sick.
Rule, Alfred	"	"	Horse lost.
Roe, Geo. W.	"	"	

Name and Rank.	Residence.	Enrolled	Remarks.
		1832.	
Sprague, Ephriam.	LaSalle Co...	June 20	Horse lost.............................
Toops, John.........	"	June 19	
Thompson, Beverly A	"	"	
Turman, John G....	"	"	
Vineyard, Squire....	"	"	
Walker, James......	"	"	Furloughed June 16 from Ft. Wilbourn, sick..
Willis, James........	"	"	

Capt. Thomas Stout's Company,

2d Regiment, 3d Brigade, of Illinois Mounted Volunteers, called into the service of the United States, on the requisition of Gen. Atkinson, by the Governor's proclamation dated ———, 1832. This company organized May 5, 1832, in Bond county, Illinois. Mustered out August 16, 1832.

Name and Rank.	Residence.	Enrolled	Remarks.
Captain.		1832.	
John Stout............	Bond Co.....	June 19	
First Lieutenant.			
John Stropton.......	"	"	Absent with leave from Prairie du Chien.....
Second Lieutenant.			
John P. Hunter......	"	"	
Sergeants.			
Austin R. Diamond..	"	"	
Lewis Kerr..........	"	"	
Andrew W. Watson.	"	"	
Wilson Carson......	"	"	Absent with leave from Pra. du Ch.; horse l'st
Corporals.			
John N. Gilham.....	"	"	
Andrew Hawn.......	"	"	Absent with leave from Ft. Hamilton July 29.
Gideon B. Gilmore..	"	"	Furloughed July 10th at Ft. Kuskenon........
Alexander Steward.	"	"	Horse lost...............................
Privates.			
Black, William......	"	"	
Bull, Duncan........	"	"	
Barlow, Joseph......	"	"	
Clanton, Chapman..	"	"	Absent with leave from Prairie du Chien.....
Conry, Andrew......	"	"	
Combs, James......	"	"	Furloughed June 22, at Ft. Wilbourn........
Combs, Westley.....	"	"	Deserted June 22, at Ft. Wilbourn..........
Cox, John..........	"	"	Discharged by order of Gen. Henry, June 22.
Downing, James....	"	"	
Ellis, Noah.........	"	"	
Ellison, Price.......	"	"	
Ellison, James......	"	"	Absent with leave from Prairie du Chien.....
Enlow, James	"	"	Discharged by order of Gen. Scott, Aug. 3...
Green, George......	"	"	
Green, James.......	"	"	Absent with leave from Prairie du Chien.....
Harper, Robert......	"	"	
Harper, James......	Putnam Co...	"	
Hastings, Sutton....	Bond Co.....	"	
Hunt, Chas. W......	"	"	Discharged by order of Gen. Scott, Aug. 3...
Hunter, Samuel.....	"	"	Attached to company 20th of June..........
James, Benjamin...	"	"	
Koonce, George.....	"	"	
Little, F. John......	"	"	
Laxton, James......	Sangamon Co	"	Absent with leave from Prairie du Chien.....
McCurty, Geo. W...	Bond Co.....	"	
Moody, Richard.....	"	"	Discharged by order of Gen. Henry June 22..
Moore, James.......	"	"	
Moore, William.....	"	"	
McAdow, Samuel N.	"	"	
Moody, John F......	"	"	
McAdams, William..	"	"	
McAdams, Wm. R...	"	"	Absent with leave from Prairie du Chien.....
Nance, Webster.....	"	"	

THIRD BRIGADE.

Name and Rank.	Residence.	Enrolled	Remarks.
		1832.	
Nelson, Calvin C	Bond Co	June 19	
Paisley, William	"	"	Discharged July 26, at Helena
Pierce, Robert B	Madison Co	"	Attached to company June 20
Pigg, Elijah	Bond Co	"	
Perdien, Joshua G	"	"	
Rice, William	"	"	
Stokes, Frederick	"	"	
Stokes, William	"	"	
Stubblefield, Lewis	"	"	Absent with leave from Ft. Hamilton Aug. 12.
Stubblefield, Wiatt	"	"	
Stubblefield, Wm	"	"	Absent with leave from Prairie du Chien
Sterling, John	"	"	
Sellers, Benjamin	"	"	
Tailor, William T	"	"	Furloughed from Ft. Hamilton Aug. 12.
White, Alexander R	"	"	
White, Thomas N	"	"	Furloughed from Ft. Wilbourn June 22

THIRD REGIMENT.

Capt. Andrew Bankson's Company

Of the 3d Regiment, 3d Brigade, of Illinois Mounted Volunteers, called into the service of the United States, on the requisition of Gen. Henry Atkinson, by the Governor's proclamation dated May 15, 1832. Mustered out August 17, 1832, by order of Brig.-Gen. Atkinson. Enlisted for 90 days.

Name and Rank.	Residence.	Enrolled	Remarks.
Captain.		1832.	
Andrew Bankson	Clinton Co	May 23	Absent with leave, July 24, 1832
First Lieutenant.			
Godfrey Ammons	"	"	Present commanding the company
Second Lieutenant.			
James J. Justice	"	"	
Sergeants.			
Henry L. Roper	"	"	Horse lost July 13, 1832
Elisha Phelps	"	"	
Allen Burton	"	"	Discharged on Surg. cert. July 21, 1832
Reubin T. Hawkins	"	"	
Corporals.			
Ephriam Phelps	"	"	
John Cartel	"	"	Disch. on Surg. cert. July 21, 1832; horse lost.
Meredith T. Nichols	"	"	On furlough; horse, etc., lost in battle
John T. Donaldson	"	"	horse lost in battle
Privates.			
Alton, James	"	"	Discharged on Surg. cert. July 21, 1832. [horse
Blevins, Elijah	"	"	Disch. July 21, 1832, in consequence of loss of
Baker, William	"	"	On furlough Aug. 12, 1832; horse lost
Barcus, John	"	"	
Bradley, Joshua T.	"	"	Lost horse July 13, 1832
Bankson, James	"	"	Absent with leave July 24, 1832; horse lost
Briggs, Andrew	"	"	
Coles, Lewis	"	"	
Dunn, Jesse	"	"	
Edmunds, Levi	"	"	
Ellis, Joel	"	"	
Finch, Joshua	"	"	On furlough Aug. 2, 1832; disch. Aug. 4
French, William	"	"	
French, Richard E.	"	"	
Gates, John	"	"	
Hurst, Benjamin	"	"	Discharged on Surg. cert. July 21
Holland, James A.	"	"	
Hill, James	"	"	On furlough Aug. 2; discharged Aug. 4, 1832
Kelly, Charles D.	"	"	
King, John	"	"	
King, Emanuel	"	"	
Lauson, James	"	"	
Logan, John B.	"	"	
Mitchell, George	"	"	
McCully, Samuel	"	"	On furlough Aug. 12; lost horse on march
Martin, Peter	"	"	
Nichols, David A.	"	"	Furloughed Aug. 12, 1832
Neely, Gilbert	"	"	
Neely, Harrison	"	"	
O'Harnett, John M.	"	"	Discharged on Surg. cert. July 10, 1832
Outhouse, James	"	"	Furloughed Aug. 12, 1832
O'Melvany, John	"	"	Sick in quarters; horse lost July 13, 1832
Parker, Hiram	"	"	Absent with leave July 26, 1832; horse lost
Petty, Anderson	"	"	
Phillips, Jesse	"	"	

THIRD BRIGADE.

Name and Rank.	Residence.	Enrolled	Remarks.
		1832.	
Phelps, Presley	Clinton Co.	May 23.	Discharged on Surg. cert. July 10
Petty, William	"	"	
Roper, John	"	"	
Rodgers, John	"	"	Absent with leave, Aug. 7, 1832; horse lost
Reeves, Thomas	"	"	
Rutledge, James	Morgan Co.	June 21.	Absent with leave Aug. 7; horse lost
Ray, Solomon	Clinton Co.	May 23.	Furloughed Aug. 12 and sick
Ray, Dabel	"	"	
Scott, William	"	"	Horse lost on forced march
Spencer, Daniel	"	"	Absent with leave Aug. 7
Segreaves, Henry	"	"	
Segreaves, William	"	"	
Short, William	"	"	
Smith, Benjamin	"	"	
Settles, Isaac	"	"	Absent with leave Aug. 7; sick
Sharp, Levi	"	"	
Talbut, William	"	"	Absent with leave July 24; horse lost
Talbee, Isaac D.	Fayette Co.	June 21.	Horse lost at Mud Lake
White, George W.	Clinton Co.	May 23.	Absent with leave July 24; horse lost
Walker, Jeremiah	"	"	
Yarborough, Amb'se	"	"	

The Clinton men started from Carlyle with six days' provisions and forage for their horses at their own expense, and the officers have not drawn any extra rations of any kind during the campaign, having only drawn one single ration for each day; the company only three rations of corn for their horses. The company was organized the 23d day of May, took up their march the 28th, and mustered into the service the 21st of June. The company being discharged, drew twelve days' rations. The officers only drew a single ration. Arrived at Fort Wilbourn on the 15th June, 1832.

(Signed,) J. T. BRADLEY.

CAPT. WM. ADAIR'S COMPANY

Of the 3d Regiment, 3d Brigade, of Illinois Mounted Volunteers, called into the service of the United States, on the requisition of Gen. Henry Atkinson, by the Governor's proclamation, dated ——, 1832. Mustered out August 17, 1832.

Name and Rank.	Residence.	Enrolled	Remarks.
		1832.	
Captains.			
David Baldridge	Perry Co.	June 26	Resigned June 26, and appointed Adjutant
William Adair	"	"	Promoted Captain June 26, from the ranks
First Lieutenant.			
Jacob Short	"	June 19	Promoted, June 19, from 2d Lieutenant
Second Lieutenant.			
John Hansford	"	"	Promoted, June 19, from private; lost tent
Sergeants.			
Wm. C. Murphy	"	June 4.	Wounded in battle; left at Prairie du Chien
Anderson Bartley	"	"	
Albert B. Murphy	"	"	Lost tent
Frederick Williams	"	"	
Corporals.			
Abraham Cokenhour	"	"	Lost horse
Benjamin Hammock	"	"	Lost horse; furloughed Aug. 8
Robert Gillehan	"	"	
James M. Hogue	"	"	Furloughed Aug. 8
Privates.			
Anderson, Alexand'r	"	"	Discharged July 15 at Winnebago; surgeon
Anderson, Berry	"	"	Disch. June 23 at Wilbourn; surgeon's certif.
Brown, James	"	"	
Brown, James C.	"	"	Furloughed Aug. 8
Brown, Payton	"	"	
Benson, Lewis	"	"	
Clark, John	"	"	Furloughed Aug. 8; lost horse
Crane, Joel	"	"	
Casey, Hiram	"	"	

Name and Rank.	Residence.	Enrolled	Remarks.
		1832.	
Crow, Robert	Perry Co	June 24.	Furloughed Aug. 8.
Dickson, John	" "	" "	Disch. June 23 at Wilbourn; surgeon's certif.
Earnest, Andrew	" "	" "	
Ford, Jesse	" "	" "	
France, Peter	" "	" "	
Garner, Francis	" "	" "	
Hawkins, Ausborn	" "	" "	
Hutchings, Eli J	" "	" "	
Hutching, ———	" "	" "	Died Aug. 3 of wounds received Aug. 2.
Hutching, William	" "	" "	Dead; left sick at Salt River June 14.
Huggins, James	" "	" "	
Hull, Zebedee	" "	" "	
Keath, Resin	" "	" "	
Keath, Bown	" "	" "	
McDowell, Thomas J	" "	" "	
Misenhammer, Pet'r	" "	" "	
Montague, James M.	" "	" "	Left sick at Prairie du Chien.
Pitchford, Samuel	" "	" "	Lost horse.
Pyle, Abner	" "	" "	Lost horse.
Petit, Jonathan	" "	" "	
Reece, Ephriam	" "	" "	
Rice, Abner L	" "	" "	
Terry, George	" "	" "	
Williams, Beverly	" "	" "	Discharged June 23 at Wilbourn.
Wells, Joseph	" "	" "	Disch. at Blue Mound, being wounded Aug. 10
Wells, Josiah	" "	" "	
Welks, Peter W	" "	" "	Furloughed Aug. 8.
Woodrum, Nicholas	" "	" "	
Washburn, John	" "	" "	
Wolf, Thomas	" "	" "	Furloughed Aug. 8.

CAPT. JOSIAH S. BRIGGS' COMPANY,

3d Regiment, 3d Brigade, of Illinois Mounted Volunteers, called into the service of the United States, on the requisition of Gen. Henry Atkinson, by the Governor's proclamation dated May 15, 1832. Mustered out August 17, 1832.

Name and Rank.	Residence.	Enrolled	Remarks.
		1832.	
Captain.			
Josiah S. Briggs	Randolph Co.	May 24	
First Lieutenant.			
John Morrison	" "	" "	
Second Lieutenant.			
John Thompson	" "	" "	Left at Winnebago with Col. Sharp; ord to Galena; horse lost.
Sergeants.			
Robert Mann	" "	" "	
Francis S. Jones	" "	" "	
John Alcorn	" "	" "	
James Harmon	" "	" "	
Corporals.			
Andrew McFarlin	" "	" "	Horse lost.
John McFarlin	" "	" "	
Richard Bradley	" "	" "	discharged at Winnebago July 15.
Samuel Hathorn	" "	" "	
Privates.			
Anderson, David	" "	" "	Supposed to be discharged at Casheonong.
Anderson, Thomas	" "	" "	
Barbour, James	" "	" "	Left to attend Saml. Barbour, sick at Ft. Win-
Batman, James	" "	" "	(nebago.
Burns, Samuel	" "	" "	
Brown, Samuel	" "	" "	
Campbell, Alexand'r	" "	" "	Furnished, July 25, Wm. Harper as substit'te;
Campbell, Samuel	" "	" "	trans. to Capt. Lindsey's Co. July 25
Caldwell, Robert	" "	" "	Left at Prairie du Chien, sick.
Christie, Eneas	" "	" "	Left with Col. Sharp at Winneb. on det. serv.
Crawford, Samuel	" "	" "	Left at Prairie du Chien, sick.

THIRD BRIGADE.

Name and Rank.	Residence.	Enrolled	Remarks.
		1832.	
Clendenen, Wm. S.	Randolph Co.	May 24	Horse lost........................
Gilbreath, Jno. R.	"	"	
Hathorn, John	"	"	Promoted Sergeant-Major June 21.
Huey, John C.	"	"	
Hughes, John M.	"	"	
Harr, Sanford	"	"	
Jernigan, Bryant B.	"	"	
Jones, Moses	"	"	
Kilpatrick, Isaac A.	"	"	Left at Fort Hamilton, sick.
Lee, James F.	"	"	
Lee, John	"	"	Horse lost........................
Lee, Thomas	"	"	
Lively, Joseph	"	"	?
Laird, John	"	"	
Lively, James	"	"	
Murphy, David	"	"	
McHenry, John	"	"	
McDill, Samuel	"	"	
Morgan, Hiram	"	"	Left to attend sick at Prairie du Chien........
Maxwell, Samuel	"	"	horse lost
Oliver, Duritt	"	"	Left at Blue Mounds, sick
Patterson, James H.	"	"	Left at Prairie du Chien, sick.
Pettitt, Samuel	"	"	
Robinson, Richard	"	"	Horse lost.
Short, Thomas J.	"	"	Killed July 21.
Smith, Francis	"	"	
Swanwick, Francis	"	"	Left to attend the sick at Prairie du Chien.
Sadler, Benjamin	"	"	
Sheets, Firman	"	"	Horse lost........................
Thomerson, George	"	"	
White, John	"	"	Wounded in battle Aug. 2, Prairie du Chien.
Woods, John	"	"	

This company enrolled and elected its officers on May 24, 1832. Marched, on May 27, 1832, for Beardstown, and was mustered into the service of the United States June 21, 1832.

CAPT. JAMES THOMPSON'S COMPANY

Of the 3d Regiment, 3d Brigade, of Illinois Mounted Volunteers, called into the service of the United States by the Governor's proclamation, dated ——, 1832. Mustered out August 17, 1832.

Name and Rank.	Residence.	Enrolled	Remarks.
		1832.	
Captain.			
James Thompson	Randolph Co.	June 4	
First Lieutenant.			
Samuel Barber	"	"	Absent, sick; left at Ft. Winnebago July 15.
Second Lieutenant.			
Wm. H. McDill	"	"	Absent; left at Prairie du Chien to take care of John White, wounded by Indians.
Sergeants.			
Moses W. Taggart	"	"	............[care of Robert Smith, sick.
Richard Lively	"	"	Absent; left above Prairie du Chien to take
Robert C. Jones	"	"	
Harmon Marlin	"	"	
Corporals.			
Archibald Crozier	"	"	
Robert Hamilton	"	"	..................[wounded by Indians.
James Thomson, Jr.	"	"	Absent; left to take care of Andr. McCormick,
William Pike	"	"	
Privates.			
Brown, John	"	"	
Brown, John C.	"	"	
Been, Allen	"	"	
Ball, Nelson	"	"	Discharged at Blue Mound on Surg. certif.
Bowerman, William	"	"	

Name and Rank.	Residence.	Enrolled	Remarks.
		1832	
Bilderback, Friend	Randolph Co.	June 4	
Crozier, Andrew	"	"	
Davis, Robert	"	"	
Dukes, Martin	"	"	
Davis, Ishom F.	"	"	
Foster, John	"	"	
Gray, William	"	"	Lost his horse on forced march
Hathaway, Harvey	"	"	
Harmon, Jacob	"	"	
Hathaway, Milton	"	"	
Hughes, John	"	"	
Jones, Andrew	"	"	
Layne, Wiley	"	"	
Milligan, James	"	"	Discharged at Blue Mound on Surg. certif.
McBride, Absalom	"	"	
McCormick, Andrew	"	"	Absent with leave; wounded in battle
Murphy, Miller	"	"	
Marlin, Edward F.	"	"	Got his horse killed
Miller, Robert	"	"	
McNeel, William	"	"	
Overton, Benj., Jr.	"	"	Present, sick
Patterson, John	"	"	Absent; left to take care of his brother James
Parks, William	"	"	Lost his horse; present, sick
Reed, James	"	"	
Short, John	"	"	Discharged at Blue Mound on Surg. certif.
Steele, James	"	"	Absent on furlough since July 25
Steele, George	"	"	Lost his horse
Smith, Robert R.	"	"	Absent, sick; left near Prairie du Chien
Taylor, John	"	"	
Thomas, John W.	"	"	
Tindel, John	"	"	
Vickers, Abel	"	"	
Wilcox, James	"	"	
Wise, Enoch G.	"	"	Horse drowned; got another, lost him

This company was raised and organized on June 4, under the command of Gabriel Jones, Captain; James Thompson, 1st Lieut.; Samuel Barber, 2d Lieut. Marched on June 8, and was mustered into the service at Fort Wilbourn June 21, under Capt. James Thompson, Gabriel Jones having been elected Colonel.

Capt. Jacob Feaman's,
afterwards
Capt. James Conner's, Company

Of the 3d Regiment, 3d Brigade, of Illinois Mounted Volunteers, called into the service of the United States, on the requisition of Gen. Atkinson, by the Governor's proclamation dated —— 1832. Mustered out August 17, 1832.

Name and Rank.	Residence.	Enrolled	Remarks.
		1832	
Captains.			
Jacob Feaman	Randolph Co.	May 25	Resigned July 25
James Conner	"	"	Promoted, July 25, from 1st Lieut. to Capt.
First Lieutenant.			
Mathew Gray	"	"	Promoted, July 25, from 1st Sergt. to Lieut.
Second Lieutenant.			
David Wright	"	"	Pro. June 7 and left sick at Prairie du Chien.
Sergeants.			
Isaac Nelson	"	"	Appointed, July 25
George Glenn	"	"	" June 22
Menard Maxwell	"	"	" 20
Joseph Orr	"	"	Quartermaster Sergeant, July 26.

Name and Rank.	Residence.	Enrolled	Remarks.
Corporals.		1832.	
Patrick Faherty	Randolph Co.	May 25.	
James Whalen	"	"	
John Levett	"	"	Supposed discharged, Aug. 4, 1832.
Wiley Paschall	"	"	Horse lost or stolen.
Privates.			
Bond, Edward	"	"	
Brewer, Vincent	"	"	
Brightwell, John	"	"	
Brown, Allanson	"	"	Discharged, June 21, disability
Bogy, Lewis V	"	"	July 15
Chapall, Elias	"	"	
Chaupine, Lewis	"	"	
Doris, Martin W	"	"	Promoted Paymaster, July 15.
Dugger, Flud	"	"	Left at Prairie du Chien to tend sick, Aug. 7.
Drousse, Henry	"	"	
Davis, Michael	"	"	
Doza, Joseph	"	"	
Evens, William	"	"	
Fulton, William	"	"	
Hampton, Wilson	"	"	[on the 25th
Jones, Armstead	"	"	Wounded on July 21, and absent with leave
Jarrel, John	"	"	
Keemasa, Baptist	"	"	
Langton, Francis	"	"	Left sick at Mounds, July 25.
Lackopelle, Henry	"	"	
Levens, Henry	"	"	
Minard, Medard	"	"	Absent with leave, Aug. 7.
Miers, James P	"	"	Detached to tend on Jones, July 25.
Mart, Ravelle	"	"	
Morrison, William	"	"	Absent with leave, Aug. 7.
Mudd, Harrison	"	"	
Minard, Peter	"	"	Lost horse and pack-saddle on forced march
Onger, Ferdinand	"	"	
O'Hara, John	"	"	Discharged, July 15; disability.
Phillips, Berrel	"	"	
Patterson, Bhenler	"	"	
Penneaua, Baptist	"	"	Horse lost on or near Four Lakes
Pascal, Francis	"	"	
Roberts, Abram	"	"	
Reynolds, John	"	"	
Seymour, Grove	"	"	Supposed discharged, July 26, 1832.
Vrain, Dometius F	"	"	Discharged, June 16; disability.
Will, Joseph	"	"	
Winter, William	"	"	
Woolsey, Wash'ton	"	"	
Wilson, David E	"	"	Left at Prairie du Chien, sick.
White, John	"	"	
Willmuth, Louis	"	"	

This company was organized at Kaskaskia, May 25, 1832, and was mustered into the service of the United States at Fort Wilbourn, June 21, 1832.

Capt. James Burns' Company

Of 3d Regiment, 3d Brigade of Mounted Volunteers, called into the service of the United States, on the requisition of Gen. Atkinson, by the Governor's proclamation dated May 15, 1832. Mustered into the service June 21, 1832. Mustered out August 17, 1832. Organized May 4, 1832.

Name and Rank.	Residence.	Enrolled	Remarks.
Captain.			
James Burns	Washing'n Co	May 4	
First Lieutenants.			
Andrew Lyons			Resigned June 28; does duty in line
William Wood			Lost horse; elected from 1st Corp. June 28; [lost tent.
Second Lieutenant.			
Cyrus Sawyers			Furl'd July 25; lost horse & tent on f'ced m'ch

Name and Rank.	Residence.	Enrolled	Remarks.
Sergeants.			
John D. Wood			Resigned June 21; promoted to Major
Henry Cherry			Absent with leave July 25
John H. Hood			Lost his horse; lost tent on forced march
Harvey Nevels			
Anthony Darter			Furloughed July 25; lost tent on forced m'ch
Corporals.			
John Mitchell			Broke bayonet
George Terrill			
Marquis G. Faulkner			Absent with leave Aug. 12; lost his horse
William Minson			Discharged July 15, on Surgeon's certificate.
Privates.			
Anderson, Samuel K.			Lost his blanket
Anderson, James			
Anderson, Alexand'r			
Andrew, Lyons			Absent with leave Aug. 12; lost his horse
Burns, John M			" " " " "
Burns, Samuel			" " " " "
Burns, Robert			" " " " "
Balch, Armstead B.			" " July 25
Casner, John			" " Aug. 12
Gilbreath, John W.			
Holly, Pleasant I. M.			
Rouse, Anthony M.			Absent with leave Aug. 5; lost his horse
Hutchens, Richard			Lost his horse; lost tent on forced march
Joiner, William			
James, Preston B.			Absent with leave July 25
King, William			" " "
Knight, John			" " Aug. 12
Lee, George W.			
Linch, Mathew K.			Absent with leave Aug. 12; lost his horse
Locke, James			" " "
Livesay, Lorenzo D.			
McMillen, Meredith S			Disch. July 25, being wounded July 21 in b'ttle
McElhannon, Jas. M.			Absent with leave July 25
Mitchell, Samuel C.			
Morgan, Solomon			
Morgan, Cary			Absent with leave July 25
Morgan, Benajah			
Pate, George W.			
Paterson, James			Absent with leave August 5
Pepper, Moseel D.			Appointed Surgeon's Mate June 21
Linyon, Edward			Absent with leave Aug. 12
Ramsey, James			
Thompson, James			Disch. July 25, being wounded July 21 in b'ttle
Tate, William			Absent; lost his horse & tent on forced m'ch.
Underwood, David			
Underwood, James			Furloughed on Surgeon's certificate June 22.
Wells, Levi			
White, James R.			
White, Andrew			
White, James S.			
Wood, Charles H.			Lost his horse

FOURTH REGIMENT.

Capt. Bennet Nowlen's Company

Of 4th Regiment, 3d Brigade, Illinois Mounted Volunteers, called into the service of the United States, on the requisition of Gen. Henry Atkinson, by the Governor's proclamation dated May 15, 1832. Mustered out August 16, 1832.

Name and Rank.	Residence.	Enrolled	Remarks.
Captain.		1832.	
Bennet Nowlen	Macoupin Co.	June 19	
First Lieutenants.			
Jesse Scott	"	"	Resigned July 10, 1832
John Yowell	"	"	Elected 1st Lieut. July 12, 1832
Second Lieutenant.			
John Allen	"	"	Furloughed August 14, 1832
Sergeants.			
Silas Harris	"	"	
George Sprouse	"	"	Discharged August 11, 1832
Cherry Peterson	"	"	
Daniel Huddlestun	"	"	
Corporals.			
Thomas McManus	"	"	Discharged August 11, 1832
Christopher Gilpin	"	"	
Thomas Grant	"	"	
Zachariah Stewart	"	"	
Privates.			
Adams, William C	"	"	
Bowford, Thomas	"	"	
Brawdy, Azariah	"	"	Furloughed June 20, 1832, on Surg. certificate.
Brown, Wiley	"	"	
Caudle, Isham	"	"	
Cummings, Thomas	"	"	
Cummings, Samuel	"	"	
Chapman, John	"	"	
Caudle, Thomas	"	"	
England, John	"	"	Horse lost
Funderburk, Titus L	"	"	
Gibson, Jacob	"	"	Discharged August 2, 1832
Hill, Wyat R	"	"	
Hutton, Charles K	"	"	
Hughs, Thomas	"	"	
Jordan, James	"	"	
Lair, Charles	"	"	Furloughed July 10, 1832
McCollum, Isaac	"	"	
McPeters, Harvy	"	"	
McKindley, Edward	"	"	
Nevins, John	"	"	Furloughed July 10, 1832
Powers, John H	"	"	
Pruet, Isaac	"	"	
Record, John	"	"	Horse lost
Richardson, Thomas	"	"	
Rush, William	"	"	Horse lost
Richards, Edmund	"	"	
Sandridge, Hasting	"	"	Furloughed August 14, 1832
Snell, Hardy	"	"	
Simmons, Joshua	"	"	

Name and Rank.	Residence.	Enrolled	Remarks.
		1832.	
Sharp, Isaac	Macoupin Co.	June 19	
Snow, Obed	"	"	
Turner, Edmund L.	"	"	
Vincent, Joseph	"	"	

Company formed and elected Powell H. Sharp Captain, Bennet Nowlen 1st Lieut., and John Allen 2d Lieut., June 9, 1832. Marched June 11, 1832. Mustered into service June 19, 1832.

Powell H. Sharp promoted Lieut.-Colonel June 19, 1832. Bennet Nowlen promoted Captain June 19, 1832.

Capt. Ozias Hail's Company,

4th Regiment, 3d Brigade, of Illinois Mounted Volunteers, called into the service of the United States, on the requisition of Gen. Henry Atkinson, by the Governor's proclamation dated May 15, 1832. Mustered out August 16, 1832.

Name and Rank.	Residence.	Enrolled	Remarks.
Captain.		1832.	
Ozias Hail	Pike Co.	June 19.	
First Lieutenant.			
David Seeley	"	"	
Second Lieutenant.			
Robart Goodin	"	"	
Sergeants.			
Enoch Cooper	"	"	
Adam Harpool	"	"	
John McMullin	"	"	
Isaac Turnbaugh	"	"	
Josiah Sims	"	"	Discharged July 21
Corporals.			
Benjamin Shin	"	"	
John Battershell	"	"	Furloughed June 23
William Cooper	"	"	
Isaac Dolbaugh	"	"	
John Crass	"	"	Discharged July 15
Privates.			
Ames, Smith	"	"	
Alcorn, William	"	"	
Blair, Culverson	"	"	
Bradshaw, Elijah	"	"	
Blythe, John	"	"	Lost his horse
Bradshaw, Enoch	"	"	" " by forced march
Burcaloo, John	"	"	
Baker, Sylvanus	"	"	
Butler, Derns	"	"	
Buffenbarger, Wm	"	"	
Butley, Frederick	Morgan Co.	"	Discharged June 22; lost his horse; wagoner
Cole, David	Pike Co.	"	" " July 15.
Clark, Abner	"	"	
Davis, Joshua	"	"	
Davis, William	"	"	
Foster, John	"	"	Left at Ft. Dickson sick; supp. disch'd Aug. 7
Franklin, Frederic	"	"	Left sick on the road June 12
Harpool, William	"	"	
Kinney, William	"	"	
McLain, Absalom	"	"	Furloughed June 23
Miller, Calep	Pike Co.	"	
Miller, George	"	"	
Moore, David	"	"	
Melhizer, John	"	"	Horse lost
McLain, Wm	"	"	Furloughed June 25
Mitchell, William	Pike Co.	"	
Neeley, Burgess	"	"	
Neeley, John	"	"	Gun bursted
Neeley, Samuel	"	"	

Name and Rank.	Residence.	Enrolled	Remarks.
		1832.	
Neeley, Thomas		June 19	Left sick at Wilbourn June 23
Nisenger, Resen	Pike Co.	"	
Prior, James B	"	"	Discharged July 15; horse lost
Pulum, Benjamin	"	"	
Shinn, John	"	"	
Spears, Harris	"	"	
Stigney, Philip H	"	"	
Turnbough, Joseph	"	"	
Taylor, John M	"	"	
Yesley, Ebenezer	"	"	

The above company volunteered and organized in Atlas, in Pike county, on June 4, 1832, and in pursuance of orders then received, marched immediately to rendezvous at Fort Wilbourn, where they arrived on June 17, and were mustered into service June 19, 1832.

CAPT. JESSE CLAYWELL'S COMPANY,

4th Regiment, 3d Brigade of Illinois Mounted Volunteers, called into the service of the United States, on the requisition of Gen. Atkinson, by the Governor's proclamation, dated May 15, 1832. Mustered out of service Aug. 16, 1832.

Name and Rank.	Residence.	Enrolled	Remarks.
Captain.		1832	
Jesse Claywell	Sangamon Co.	June 5.	Furloughed at Wisconsin river July 27.
First Lieutenants.			
John H. Wilcoxson	"	"	Elected 1st Lieut. July 11; sick at Hamilton
Lowyel Cox	"	"	Resigned July 10
Second Lieutenant.			
Rezen H. Constant	"	"	Elected 2d Lieutenant July 11
Sergeants.			
Archibald Cass	"	"	Elected 1st Sergeant July 11
Andrew Moore	"	"	
Valentine R. Mallory	"	"	At Fort Crawford
William S. Hussey	"	"	Attending to a sick man
Corporals.			
Nathan Hussey, 1st	"	"	Prom. Brig. Wagon Master June 21; lost horse
Robert L. Gott, 1st	"	"	Attending to a sick man at Hamilton
William B. Hagan, 2d	"	"	
James C. Hagan, 3d	"	"	
Harris'n McGary, 4th	"	"	Transferred to Capt. Earley's Co. June 20
John McLemoor, 4th	"	"	
Privates.			
Anderson, Alexand'r	"	"	
Anderson, Lewis C	"	"	
Anderson, James	"	"	
Anderson, Wash'ton	"	"	
Burns, John R	"	"	
Barnet, William I	"	"	
Barnet, William	"	"	
Barnet, Hugh	"	"	
Brewer, John, Sr	"	"	Furloughed July 10; also lost his horse
Brewer, John, Jr	"	"	
Cass, Anderson B	"	"	
Constant, Nathan E	"	"	
Constant, Isaac	"	"	
Crocker, Harvey	"	"	
Currey, George	"	"	
Copeland, John	"	"	
Dooley, Jeremiah	"	"	Discharged July 27 for disability
Dement, William	"	"	Lost horse, saddle and bridle
Elliott, Haddon	"	"	Furloughed by the Surgeon's certificate
Elliott, Richard	"	"	
Glenn, David A	"	"	
Green, George	"	"	

Name and Rank.	Residence.	Enrolled	Remarks.
		1832.	
Helm, Guy	Sangamon Co	June 5.	
Hagan, Samuel C.	"	"	
Hide, John	"	"	
Kelly, Jeremiah	"	"	Lost horse, saddle and bridle
Langston, James	"	"	
Lucas, Thomas	"	"	
McGary, Hugh	"	"	Transferred to Capt. Earley's Co. June 20.
Martin, Joseph	"	"	
Neucam, William T.	"	"	
Pickerel, Benj. F.	"	"	Transferred to Capt. Earley's Co. June 20.
Prim, Abraham	"	"	
Powel, John	"	"	
Powel, Hiram	"	"	Furloughed at Ft. Wilbourn June 20.
Rogers, William F.	"	"	Lost his horse.
Riddle, James	"	"	
Snelson, John W.	"	"	
Shearley, James	"	"	
Smith, Joseph I.	"	"	
Smith, Philip	"	"	
Smith, Eliphas	"	"	Furloughed at Ft. Wilbourn June 20.
Stone, William A.	"	"	
Stone, Caleb	"	"	
Turner, William	"	"	
Waldon, James	"	"	
Wilcox, Ephriam	"	"	
Young, Joseph R.	"	"	Wound'd in battle at Mississ.; at Ft. Crawford

This company was organized June 5, 1832, marched for place of rendezvous on June 10, and was mustered into service June 20, 1832.

Capt. Reuben Brown's Company

Of 4th Regiment, 3d Brigade, Mounted Illinois Volunteers, called into the service of the United States, on the requisition of Gen. Atkinson, by the Governor's proclamation, dated May 15, 1832. Mustered out Aug. 16, 1832.

Name and Rank.	Residence.	Enrolled	Remarks.
Captain.		1832	
Reuben Brown	Sangamon Co	June 20.	Commanding company; present, but sick
First Lieutenant.			
William Baker	"	"	
Second Lieutenant.			
Daloss Brown	"	"	On furlough during term enrollment, in con-[sequence of a wound.
Sergeants.			
Thomas Jones	"	"	
Saml. E. McKenzey	"	"	Promoted from private to Sergt. June 19, 1832.
Evan Morgan	"	"	Furl. during term of enroll.; cause, sickness.
Nathan Said	"	"	Furloughed Aug. 7, 1832, during term service.
Corporals.			
Jesse Said	"	"	
Benson Brown	"	"	
John Fegan	"	"	
James B. Jones	"	"	
Privates.			
Archer, Winston	"	"	
Baker, Thomas	"	"	
Baker, James	"	"	
Brown, Jerry	"	"	
Cutright, Peter	"	"	Joined from Capt. Warwick's Co. of Mounted
Durboin, Edward	"	"	[Volunteers Aug. 1, 1832, per certificate.
Delay, Stephen	"	"	
Duglass, Thomas	"	"	Furloughed Aug. 7, 1832, during term service.
Donaldson, Dudley	"	"	
Hendricks, Samuel	"	"	
Huggard, James	"	"	Furloughed Aug. 12, 1832, during term service.

THIRD BRIGADE. 77

Name and Rank.	Residence.	Enrolled	Remarks.
		1832	
Larkin, Young	Sangamon Co	June 20	
Lucas, Allen B	"	"	
Lucas, James	"	"	Deserted June 22, 1832, from Ft. Wilbourn, Ill.
Morgan, Thomas	"	"	
Martin, Rolley	"	"	Furl. during term of service; cause, sickness
McKinzey, Henry	"	"	
Pillman, James	"	"	
Poor, James H	"	"	Lost horse in service
Pike, John	"	"	
Porter, William	"	"	On furlough Aug. 7, during term of service
Read, James	"	"	Deserted June 22, 1832, from Ft. Wilbourn, Ill.
Spillars, Wm. H	"	"	Horse lost in service; furloughed August 7,
St. John, Joseph	"	"	.........[during term of service.
Stafford, Daniel S	"	"	
Trotter, George	"	"	
Williams, Isiah B	"	"	
Transferred.			
Baker, James	"	"	Trans. June 22, 1832, to Capt. Earley's Co

This company was organized in Sangamon county, Springfield, June 6, 1832. Arrived at headquarters, Ft. Wilbourne, June 15, 1832. Mustered into service June 20, 1832.

Capt. Thomas Moffett's Company,

4th Regiment, 3d Brigade, of Illinois Mounted Volunteers, called into the service of the United States on the requisition of Gen. H. Atkinson, by the Governor's proclamation. Mustered out August 16, 1832.

Name and Rank.	Residence.	Enrolled	Remarks.
Captain.		1832.	
Thomas Moffett	SangamonCo.	June 4.	Lost his horse
First Lieutenants.			
David Black	"	"	Resigned and went home July 10
Shadrack Campbell	"	"	Elected vice D. Black, resigned July 10, 1832
Second Lieutenant.			
James Watson	"	"	
Sergeants.			
John Oldfield	"	"	Lost his horse
Thos. Epperson	"	"	Elected vice Joseph Inslee; resigned July 10.
Joseph Inslee	"	"	Discharged by Gen. Atkinson June 29
George Lindsey	"	"	Elected vice T. Epperson; resigned July 10
Franklin Williams	"	"	Lost his horse
Wm. C. Stephenson	"	"	
Corporals.			
John Humphreys	"	"	
James Campbell	"	"	Horse lost
Nathan Ralston	"	"	
Jarret McKinney	"	"	
Cornet.			
Gersham Dorrence	"	"	
Saddler.			
John Ridgeway	"	"	
Farrier.			
Jesse H. Steel	"	"	
Trumpeter.			
Armstead Ables	"	"	Discharged by Gen. Atkinson July 10
David Duncan	"	"	Elected July 10 vice Armstead Ables, disch'd.
Privates.			
Armstrong, Hugh M.	"	"	
Atkinson, Bushrod	"	"	Furloughed August 11
Brazzle, William	"	"	

Name and Rank.	Residence.	Enrolled	Remarks.
		1832.	
Ball, Smith	Sangam'n Co.	June 4.	
Crain, Thomas	"	"	Discharged July 10 by Gen. Atkinson
Cooper, William	"	"	
Carmar, Walter	"	"	
Cabaniss, Zabulon P.	"	"	
Durham, Walter	"	"	
Duncan, Joseph W.	"	"	
Drennan, A. P.	"	"	Furloughed August 11
Elkin, Garret	"	"	June 18
Epperson, Thomas	"	"	Served as 2d Sergeant from June 29 to July 10
Enix, James	"	"	Lost one U. S. pistol
Forbas, R. A.	"	"	
Getsondiner, Jno. L.	"	"	
Glascock, Gregory	"	"	Lost his horse
Hill, John P.	"	"	Lost his horse
Latham, John	"	"	Furloughed on account of sickness June 19
Lowe, Richard	"	"	
Levi, John	"	"	Descended the Miss. river Aug. 8
Lane, Jacob	"	"	Horse missing
Langley, Robert	"	"	
McAllister, William	"	"	
Moore, Joseph	"	"	
Milts, William	"	"	
Norris, Joseph	"	"	
Paine, Barzilla	"	"	
Pulliam, Martin G.	"	"	Furloughed June 20 on account of sickness
Pierce, Philctus G.	"	"	Lost his horse
Peter, Samuel	"	"	Absent without leave June 23
Saunders, Presley	"	"	
Smith, Tillman	"	"	
Smith, John	"	"	Furloughed June 27 on account of sickness
Smith, Adam	"	"	Joined D. Earley's Spy company June 29
Stout, George	"	"	
Watson, Hiram	"	"	Lost his horse
Warnsing, John	"	"	Promoted Reg'l Surg. Mate June 22; horse lost

This company mustered into the service at Fort Wilbourn June 20, 1832; was enrolled and mustered preparatory to starting from home at Springfield, Ill., June 4, 1832.

Capt. Henry L. Webb's Company

Of Mounted Volunteers, called into the service of the United States by order of the Governor of the State, by his order of the 15th of May, 1832, until 3d August, 1832, when mustered out of service by order of Major-General Scott, commanding Northwestern army.

Name and Rank.	Residence.	Enrolled	Remarks.
Captain.		1832.	
Henry L. Webb	Alex'nder Co.	May 19	
First Lieutenant.			
Richard H. Price	"	"	Rifle lost swimming Rock River after Indians
Second Lieutenants.			
David H. Moore	"	"	Promoted Qu'rmaster Spy Bat. 3d Br. June 16
James D. Morris	"	June 16	Elected 2d Lt. June 16, when comm'n'd Corp. from the 19th of May, '32, until promoted
Sergeants.			
Owen Willis, 1st	"	May 19	
Quinton Ellis, 2d	"	"	
Aaron Atherton, Jr., 3	"	"	
Sam. Ath'ton Neal, 4th	"	"	
Corporals.			
Merritt Howell	"	"	
Aaron Anglin	"	"	
William Dickey	"	"	
Giles Whitaker	"	"	

THIRD BRIGADE. 79

Name and Rank.	Residence.	Enrolled	Remarks.
Privates.		1832.	
Anglin, William	Alex'nder Co.	May 19	
Anglin, James	"	"	
Bunch, Cader	"	"	
Burks, Hardin	"	"	
Brown, Berry	"	"	
Brooks, Benj	"	"	
Caines, John	"	"	
Cannon, Tillman	"	"	
Dexter, Jeremiah	"	"	
Daniels, Solomon	"	"	
Eckols, Benjamin	"	"	
Harrison, Henry H.	"	"	
Harvill, Loudy	"	"	
Hargis, Resin	"	"	
Hughs, Franklin	"	"	
Hurgis, Turner	"	"	
Jeffers, John E.	"	"	Absent with leave
Johnson, Henry K.	"	"	
Keneda, Thomas	"	"	
Keneda, Alexander	"	"	
Lackey, Alfred	"	"	
Lynch, Cyrus S.	"	"	Rifle lost swim'ing Rock River after Indians.
McCool, George	"	"	
McCool, Benjamin	"	"	
Meshow, William	"	"	
McCloud, Roderick	"	"	
Murphy, John	"	"	
Neale, George C.	"	"	
Post, Marcus	"	"	
Phillips, James	"	"	
Rice, Samuel F.	"	"	
Powell, Wm. S.	"	"	
Powell, Alanson	"	"	Prom. Q. M. Sergt. Spy Bat. 3d Brig. June 16.
Russell, Robert	"	"	
Smith, Enoch	"	"	
Taylor, James M.	"	"	
Thompson, Nathan M	"	"	
Townsend, James W.	"	"	
Townsend, John	"	"	
White, Samuel	"	"	

SPY BATTALION.

Capt. Allen F. Lindsey's Company

Of the Spy Battalion, 3d Brigade, Illinois Mounted Volunteers, called into service of the United States, on the requisition of Gen. Atkinson, by the Governor's proclamation dated May 16, 1832. Mustered out August 16, 1832.

Name and Rank.	Residence.	Enrolled	Remarks.
Captain.		1832.	
Allen F. Lindsey	Morgan Co	June 19	Horse unfit for service, by forced marching.
First Lieutenant.			
William Scott	"		Sick in tent
Second Lieutenant.			
Isaac R. Bennett	"		One sorrel mare lost by forced marching
Sergeants.			
Martin Harding	"		One bay mare lost in service
Leftridge B. Lindsey	"		
Geo. W. Beggs	"		One bayonet scabbard lost in service
David Thomsberry	"		Furloughed July 25th at Casleman
Corporals.			
John Caldwell	"		One bayonet lost in service
Thos. R. Thompson	"		
John A. Creed	"		One mare lost on forced march; one bayonet-
Royal Flynn	"		[belt and scabbard.
Privates.			
Cox, Thomas	"		
Cooper, William			
Cumins, William	Sanganaw Cy		
Dick, John P	Morgan Co		Detailed by Brig. Qr. Master July 4, 1832
Fox, Madison	"		
Flynn, William	"		
Flynn, Zadock W	"		One bay mare lost in service
Garrett, Jesse B	"		Furloughed July 25th at Casleman
Hudspoth, John	"		
Hash, Philip	"		One bay horse and bayonet lost in service
Harper, William	"		Transferred from Capt. Biggs' Co. July 25th
King, Daniel	Sanganaw Cy	June 22	
Lindsey, William	Morgan Co		
Lucas, William	"	June 22	One bay mare lost in service
Lucas, John	"		
Mathews, William	"		Furloughed July 25th at Casleman
Meeker, Usel	Sanganaw Cy	June 22	
Manchester, David	Morgan Co		
McDonald, Frederi'k	"	June 22	On detailed service
Olaker, Jacob	"		
Ogle, James A	"		
Plaster, Thomas	"		On detached service by Gov., July 4, 1832
Paschel, Samuel	"		
Poindexter, Micajah	"		Sick in tent; horse rendered unfit for service.
Ritchie, William	"		
Sims, Westley	"		[at Dixon's Ferry.
Shelton, David	Morgan Co		Discharged June 27, 1832, by Com.-in-Chief.
Taylor, James	"		Furloughed July 25th at Casleman
Thomas, James J	"		
Woldridge, Thomas	"		Absent with leave
Walker, James H	"		Mare, bayonet and scabbard lost in service
Yaple, Jacob	"		

This company was organized June 4, and was mustered into service on June 19.

Capt. Samuel Huston's Company,

Spy Battalion, 3d Brigade, of Illinois Mounted Volunteers, called into the service of the United States, on the requisition of Gen. Henry Atkinson, by the Governor's proclamation dated May 15, 1832. Mustered out Aug. 16, 1832, by order of Brig.-Gen. Atkinson.

Name and Rank.	Residence.	Enrolled	Remarks.
Captain.		1832.	
Samuel Huston	Fayette Co.	June 7.	
First Lieutenant.			
John Wetwood	"	"	Left Helena July 27; lost his horse July 23.
Second Lieutenant.			
Henry Brown	"	"	
Sergeants.			
Payton R. Bankson	"	"	
Richard Auston	"	"	Lost his horse on the 11th of August
Hezekiah Thompson	"	"	
Isaac Fancher	"	"	Lost his horse on the 7th of August
Corporals.			
Benjamin Seals	"	"	Left sick on the 27th of July
Andrew I. Hickerson	"	"	
Alexander Fancher	"	"	Lost his horse on the 7th of August
Thomas Osbrooks	"	"	
Privates.			
Allen, John	"	"	
Austin, Philip L.	"	"	Furloughed at Helena on the 27th
Berry, Benjamin F.	"	"	
Beck, Paul	"	"	
Braswell, Richard	"	"	
Beal, James	"	"	
Browning, Harmon	"	"	Lost his horse on the 12th of August
Beasley, John	"	"	July
Brocket, Michael	"	"	
Browning, Joseph	"	"	
Baley, Henry P	"	"	
Blundell, James	"	"	Left at Helena
Carson, James	"	"	
Cole, Eldridge	"	"	
Carter, Joseph	"	"	Sick in camp
Coventry, John W.	"	"	
Davis, Levi	"	"	Furloughed on the 24th of July
Doyle, A. P. H.	"	"	Sick in camp
Duncan, Thomas	"	"	
Enos, Charles	"	"	Lost his horse on the 16th of July
Flemming, Mordica	"	"	10th of August
Freman, James	"	"	
Flemming, John	"	"	
Griffith, John	"	"	
Gillmore, Robert	"	"	
Herrington, John	"	"	Substituted for Wm. Linley from July 10
Hinton, Lewis	"	"	Furloughed on the 10th of July
Hickerson, Wash'n	"	"	
Hawkins, John B.	"	"	Left at Dixon in service
Harris, Zachariah	"	"	Furloughed on the 10th of July
Harris, Henry	"	"	
Johnson, Adaman	"	"	Lost his horse on the 27th of July
Jackson, William	"	"	
Kirkendal, William	"	"	Left at Helena on the 27th of July
Lawton, Henry	"	"	
Linley, William	"	"	Discharged by substitute on the 10th of July.
Lowder, Gideon	"	"	
Lee, William H.	"	"	Left sick at Helena on the 27th of July
Miller, Henry	"	"	
Micks, John S.	"	"	Left in service at Dixon
McQuinter, Alex	"	"	Furloughed on the 15th of July
Moore, Benjamin D.	"	"	
Nichols, William	"	"	
Neely, Bowling	"	"	
Pitcher, Payton I.	"	"	Lost his horse August 14
Porter, James	"	"	
Patten, James	"	"	
Parkhurst, Elijah	"	"	
Powell, Semore R.	"	"	
Prater, Alexander	"	"	

Name and Rank.	Residence.	Enrolled	Remarks.
Porter, Washington	Fayette Co	1832. June 7.	
Raybourn, Mitchell	"	"	
Remon, Frederick	"	"	Appointed Paymaster on July 10
Sears, John	"	"	
Smith, Jordan	"	"	
Smith, Henry	"	"	Lost his horse on the 14th of August
Smith, William	"	"	
Thompson, William	"	"	Lost horse on the 2d of July
Talby, James	"	"	
Trapp, John	"	"	
Welch, John	"	"	
Wakefield, John A.	"	"	
Wood, Anson	"	"	

Approved:

(Signed.)

H. ATKINSON,
Brig.-Gen. U. S. A.

This company was organized June 7, 1832, and received marching orders on the same day, and marched on the 9th and arrived at Fort Wilbourn on the 16th of June, and mustered into service June 19. This company found their own rations in full from the 8th to the 17th of June. Since the 17th of June till the present August 15th the company has found nearly all the small rations for itself.

This company was organized under the command of Capt. Wm. L. D. Ewing, at its first organization.

WHITESIDES' BRIGADE.

Regiments, Battalions and Companies commanded by Brigadier-General Samuel Whitesides.

FIRST REGIMENT.

CAPT. JULIUS L. BARNSBACK'S COMPANY

Of Mounted Volunteers, of the 1st Regiment of the Brigade under the command of Gen. Samuel Whitesides. Mustered out of the service of the United States at the mouth of Fox river, Illinois, May 28, 1832, distant 284 miles from the place of enrollment.

Name and Rank.	Residence.	Enrolled	Remarks.
Captain. Julius L. Barnsback.	Madison Co. Edwardsville.	1832. April 18	On furlough from May 18....................
First Lieutenant. Ryland Ballard......	"	"	In command of company from May 18 to 28..
Second Lieutenant. Jesse Bartlett........	"	"	....
Sergeants.			
Jacob Kinder........	"	"	On furlough, sick...........................
Mathias Hanlan.....	"	"	On furlough.................................
Stephen Gaskill.....	"	"	....
Henry Armstrong...	"	"	On furlough, horse hunting...............
Corporals.			
Robert Murphy......	"	"	On furlough.................................
John E. Sharp.......	"	"	....
Isham M. Gillham...	"	"	....
Isaac McLane.......	"	"	....
Privates.			
Armstrong, William.	"	"	On furlough, horse hunting...............
Armstrong, David...	"	"	....
Bartlett, Martin S...	"	"	Elected 1st Sergeant May 22, 1832........
Bartlett, Nicholas...	"	"	....
Barnsback, George.	"	"	....
Bowles, Austin.....	"	"	....
Bowles, Stephen....	"	"	Absent on furlough.........................
Burge, William......	"	"	....
Colyer, Charles......	"	"	Elected 4th Sergeant May 22, 1832........
Cox, Jacob B........	"	"	Absent, horse hunting.....................
Dove, John..........	"	"	....
Day, Fauntleroy....	"	"	....
Ford, Aaron.........	"	"	Absent, sick.................................
Flinn, Joseph........	"	"	....
Guthrie, Henry.....	"	"	....

Name and Rank.	Residence.	Enrolled	Remarks.
Gillham, John F.	Madison Co. Edwardsville.	1832. April 18	
Hart, Henry	"	"	
Hart, John	"	"	
Hamilton, William	"	"	
Hood, Aaron	"	"	
Johnson, Charles W.	"	"	
Johns, James	"	"	Absent, sick
Knight, James	"	"	
Kell, William	"	"	
Merry, David W.	"	"	
Motley, Obediah C.	"	"	
Norman James	"	"	Absent, horse hunting
Page, Robert	"	"	
Ralph, William	"	"	
Seybold, Samuel	"	"	On furl., sick; appointed Ass't Q. M. April 28.
Scanland, Lewis W.	"	"	
Smith, Levi	"	"	
Smith, E. C.	"	"	
Semple, James	"	"	Appointed Judge Advocate May 1, 1832.
Van Hoozer, John	"	"	
Wall, John A	"	"	
Wall, David	"	"	
Weeks, Robert B.	"	"	

Capt. John Thomas' Company

Of the 1st Regiment, commanded by Col. John Thomas, of the Brigade of Mounted Volunteer Militia from St. Clair county, Illinois, commanded by Brig.-Gen. Samuel Whitesides. Mustered out of the service of the United States, at the mouth of Fox river, Illinois, on May 28, 1832; distant 300 miles from the place of enrollment.

Name and Rank.	Residence.	Enrolled	Remarks.
Captains.		1832.	
John Thomas	Belleville	April 18.	Elected Col. of 1st Regt. on April 28
First Lieutenant.			
Gideon Simpson	"	"	Elected Capt. on April 28
Second Lieutenants.			
George Kinney	"	"	
Wm. S. Thomas	"	"	Elected 1st Lieut. on April 28
Sergeants.			
John W. Woods	"	"	Absent on furlough since May 19
Parker Adams	"	"	Elected 1st Sergt. since May 19
Prettyman Boyce	"	"	
James Nearen	"	"	
Enoch Bridges	"	"	
Corporals.			
John McDonald	"	"	
Andrew Terry	"	"	
James H. Ashby	"	"	
George West	"	"	
Privates.			
Abbott, Isaac			
Bird, John			
Casterline, Joseph O			
Crocker, Abner			Absent without leave
Davis, James			
Enochs, Saml. B.			
Furgerson, Robt			
McHenry, Daniel			Joined the 4th Regt.; returned
Ogle, Benjamin			

Name and Rank.	Residence.	Enrolled	Remarks.
		1832.	
Roman, Richard	Belleville	April 18.	Appointed Surgeon in 1st Regt. on April 28...
Spann, Solomon			
Scott, Benjamin			
Scott, Chas			
Twiss, Wm			
Welker, Jos			

Daniel McHenry returned and served out his time in my Company.
        (Signed.)   GIDEON SIMPSON, Capt.

Capt. John Tate's Company

Of Independent Riflemen of the 1st Regiment of the Mounted Brigade of Volunteers commanded by Brigadier-General Samuel Whitesides, in the service of the United States. Mustered out of service at the mouth of Fox river, Illinois, on May 28, 1832. Distance, 330 miles from the place of enrollment.

Name and Rank.	Residence.	Enrolled	Remarks.
Captain.	Belleville.		
John Tate	St. Clair Co	April 18	
First Lieutenant.			
Joshua Hughes			
Second Lieutenant.			
Abram B. Vandigrif			
Sergeants.			
Jacob Miller			
Joseph Ogle			
William Tate			
George W. Hook			
Corporals.			
James Phillips			
Jacob Phillips			
William Woods			
Mathew Cox			
Privates.			
Ashlock, Robert			
Aspons, Charles			
Bear, Peter B			
Bear, Bonham			
Blair, James			
Charles, James N			
Dunlap, John			
Dingle, Atason			
Dun, Peter			
Edwards, I. C			
Glass, George			
Higgins, Robert			
Higgins, Ichabod			Absent sick
Holt, Christopher			
Hootes, Samuel			
Hootes, Anthony			Absent on furlough, sick
Leach, Robert			Absent with brother
Leach, A. H			Absent, wounded
Lyndon, Jefferson			
Lindon, Joseph			
McClintock, James			
Miller, Absalom			Absent without leave, May 1, 1832
Million, John			
Owens, Hopson			
Owens, Charles			Absent, sick
Owens, Ellit			
Phillips, Wm			
Patason, Horland			

Name and Rank.	Residence.	Enrolled	Remarks.
Perce, George			
Powers, James			
Rader, James			
Sample, James			
Skinner, Akerman			
Swillevant, Francis			
Smith, John			
Starkey, John			Promoted Major of 2d Batt. 1st Regt., April 28
Wood, Samuel			

Capt. Josiah Little's Company

Of the 1st Regiment, commanded by Col. John Thomas, of the Brigade of Mounted Volunteers of Illinois Militia, commanded by Brig.-Gen. Samuel Whitesides. Mustered out of the service of the United States at the mouth of Fox river, Illinois, on May 27, 1832. Distance from Madison county, place of enrollment, 284 miles.

Name and Rank.	Residence.	Enrolled	Remarks.
Captains.	Alton.	1832.	
Solomon Pruitt	Madison Co.	April 19.	Elected Capt. Apr. 19; elected Lt.-Col. Apr. 28
Josiah Little	"	"	
First Lieutenants.			
Josiah Little	"	"	Elected Captain April 28, 1832
William Arundell	"	"	
Second Lieutenant.			
Jacob Swegart	"	"	On furlough
Sergeants.			
Wm. Arundell	"	"	Elected 1st Lieut. April 28, 1832
Joseph Squire	"	"	" 1st Sergt. " " On furlough.
James R. Wood	"	"	
James Sanders	"	"	Sick and not present
Corporals.			
Thomas Akins	"	"	
John E. Hawkins	"	"	
Jno. Lawrence	"	"	
Isaiah Dunagan	"	"	
Privates.			
Barnet, Benj. F			
Bridges, Madison			
Busy, Newton			On permit
Beck, Sandford			
Barr, Zachariah			
Chapman, Enoch			
Chapman, Jos.			
Cochran, Wm. C.			
Davis, William			On permit
Dickson, Thomas			
Dunagan, Jno. M.			
Edwards, Cyrus			
Eaves, William			On furlough
Ficu, James			
Gillham, Marcus			On furlough
Gillham, Josiah R			
Harris, Meeds A.			
Hodges, James H.			
Humes, Willis			
Harkleroad, Jno.			
Job, Samuel			
Job, Levi			On permit
Jones, Martin			
Jones, George			
Kirkendall, Wm.			
Kinyan, Edward			Sick and on permit
Linton, James			
Lee, Vincent			2d Sergt. April 28, 1832
More, Abel			On furlough
Pruitt, Solomon, Jr.			

Name and Rand.	Residence.	Enrolled	Remarks.
Palmer, Sam'l			
Roberts, Absalom			
Roberts, Elijah			
Rice, Elias			
Rose, Francis			
Roberts, Wm., Jr.			
Rogers, Jonathan			
Sanders, Shadrick			
Starkey, Russell			On permit
Lowell, Lewis C.			Sick and not present
Scarittlin, Stephen			
Sewill, Wm.			Detailed to wait on sick
Smith, Elias			
Stent, Christopher			
Solomon, John			
Sterell, James			4th Sergt. to May 18; 1st from that time to 27
Suels (?), William			
Wood, Jesse			3d Sergeant May 18, 1832
Walker, Philip V.			
Waddle, James			Sick and on permit
Whitesides, Thomas			

SECOND REGIMENT.

Capt. Thomas Chapman's Company

Of 2d Regiment, of the Brigade of Mounted Volunteers commanded by Brig.-Gen. Samuel Whitesides. Mustered out of service of the United States at the mouth of Fox river, on the Illinois river, in the State of Illinois, 250 miles from the place of enrollment in Greene county, on the 25th day of May, 1832.

Name and Rank.	Residence.	Enrolled	Remarks.
Captains.		1832.	
Charles Gregory	Greene Co	April 20.	[when elected Lieut.-Col. of 2d Regt. Commanded Co. from April 20 to April 30, 1832.
Thomas Chapman	"	"	Elected Captain April 30, 1832
First Lieutenant.			
Thomas Hill	"	"	Elected 1st Lieutenant April 30, 1832
Second Lieutenant.			
Levi Whitesides	"	"	Elected 2d Lieutenant April 30, 1832
Sergeants.			
Sherman Goss	"	"	Appointed 1st Sergeant April 30, 1832
Isaac Moore	"	"	" April 20, 1832
Henry Phillips	"	"	" April 30, 1832
Aaron Hart	"	"	" April 30, 1832
Corporals.			
Michael Hendrick	"	"	Appointed April 20, 1832
Samuel M. Pinkerton	"	"	" April 20, 1832
John F. Hart	"	"	" April 30, 1832
James H. Finley	"	"	
Privates.			
Burns, Martin	"	"	
Dunn, Squire	"	"	
Duff, John	"	"	Absent on furlough
Duff, Daniel	"	"	
Elmer, Elijah	"	"	
Elmore, George I.	"	"	
Elmore, Ralph	"	"	
Elmore, George R.	"	"	Absent on furlough
Garrison, Richard	"	"	
Gilleland, James	"	"	
Gilleland, William	"	"	
Hazlewood, George	"	"	
Hazlewood, Wyatt	"	"	
Philips, Israel	"	"	
Rule, Albert	"	"	Absent sick
Shelton, William	"	"	
Spencer, James R.	"	"	Sick and on furlough
Welch, Robert	"	"	
Wood, James	"	"	
Wiggins, Laban	"	"	

All the company were present except those marked absent and furloughed.

Capt. Levi D. Boone's Company

Of the 2d Regiment, commanded by Col. Jacob Fry, of the Brigade of Mounted Volunteers commanded by Brig.-Gen. Samuel Whitesides. Mustered out of the service of the United States at the mouth of Fox river, on the Illinois river, on May 28, 1832. Distance from place of enrollment, 210 miles.

Name and Rank.	Residence.	Enrolled	Remarks.
Captain.		1832.	
Levi D. Boone	Montg'm'y Co	April 20	
First Lieutenant.			
James G. Hinman			
Second Lieutenant.			
Absalom Cross			
Sergeants.			
C. G. Blackberger			
Michael H. Walker			
Israel Foogleman			
William M. David			Absent on furlough
Corporals.			
John Prater			
Alex. T. Williams			
C. S. Coffey			
Newton Street			
Privates.			
Brown, James			
Briggs, Samuel L.			Absent on furlough
Brown, Harrison			
Blair, Cobbert			
Bennett, H. C.			Quartermaster
Cress, Peter			
Canins, G. W.			
Crabtree, John			
Duff, George F.			
Fanin, Michael			Lost a rifle-gun in service, appraised at $18
Griffith, William			
Grisham, James			
Hampton, Johnson			Absent by permission, to hunt horse
Hawkins, James			
Halbrock, Benjamin			
Hunt, Joshua			
Ishmael, Sam			
Jordan, William			
Knapp, Artisua H.			
Killpatrick, Eph.			
Killingworth, Steph'n			
Ludwick, George F.			
Long, Robert A.			
McWilliams, John K.			
Mansfield, Thos. J.			
Mayfield, William			
Michael, Barnabus			
Peacock, Samuel			
Rabb, Eli			
Rutledge, James M.			
Roberts, William			
Sherley, William D.			
Steel, Daniel			
Scrivener, Curtis			
Toedd, Thomas J.			
Turner, McKensic			
Williams, James B.			
Whitton, Easton			
Williams, Ben. R.			
Young, James			

Ben. R. Williams was discharged at Beardstown April 27, 1832, and not Hawkins. Williams was discharged solely because his horse was lost, and not for any offense or misconduct.

(Signed.)   LEVI D. BOONE, Capt.

CAPT. WM. G. FLOOD'S COMPANY

Of Mounted Volunteers, of the 2d Regiment of the Brigade commanded by Brigadier General Samuel Whitesides. Mustered out of service of the United States at the mouth of Fox river, in the State of Illinois, on the 28th day of May, 1832. Distance, two hundred and fifty (250) miles from place of enrollment.

Name and Rank.	Residence.	Enrolled	Remarks.
Captain.		1832.	
Wm. G. Flood	Quincy	April 23	
First Lieutenant.			
Edward L. Pearson	"	"	
Second Lieutenant.			
Thomas Crocker	"	"	
Sergeants.			
Nathan Stringfield	"	"	On furlough
Granville Turner	"	"	
George W. Pollard	"	"	
Samuel E. Pierce	"	"	
Corporals.			
Richard S. Green	"	"	
Wm. Watson	"	"	
Elza D. Park	"	"	
John McDaniel	"	"	Sick and absent, by leave
Privates.			
Allen, Meredith	"	"	
Ames, Orestus	"	"	
Ames, Loring	"	"	
Bancroft, Amos	"	"	
Beebee, Erastus	"	"	
Browning, O. H	"	"	
Brown, George	"	"	
Boling, Lewis	"	"	
Beebee, David	"	"	
Burlingham, Sanford	"	"	
Caxe, George W	"	"	
Clark, James O	"	"	
Caldwell, John	"	"	
Doty, John	"	"	
Fortune, William	"	"	
Freeman, Elam S	"	"	Appointed Adjutant 2d Regiment
Ferguson, Isaac	"	"	Absent on duty
Howard, John	"	"	Sick and absent
Holmes, Hiram	"	"	
Johnson, Thomas	"	"	
Kinney, Thos	"	"	Sick and absent; joined Co. at Yellow banks.
Laughland, J. W	"	"	
Lightfoot, Washint'n	"	"	
Malone, Andy	"	"	
Mast, Michael	"	"	
Miller, Henry W	"	"	
Moore, Daniel	"	"	
Pond, Hiram	"	"	
Parker, Samuel	"	"	
Popple, Simeon	"	"	
Pierce, Joshua	"	"	
Ralston, J. H	"	"	Absent on duty
Richardson, William	"	"	
Sheney, John	"	"	
Seehorn, Wiley V	"	"	
Shaw, Wm	"	"	Absent by sickness
Smith, Lewis M	"	"	
Streeter, Solomon	"	"	
Turner, Ebenezer	"	"	
Thompson, James	"	"	
Warrick, Jacob	"	"	
Wood, John	"	"	
Williams, Archibald	"	"	
Wilmot, Ben. R	"	"	

CAPT. BENJAMIN JAMES' COMPANY.

Of the 2d Regiment, of Mounted Volunteers, commanded by Brig.-Gen. Samuel Whitesides. Mustered into the service of the United States at Beardstown, Illinois, on the 28th day of April, 1832, and mustered out of service on the 28th day of May, 1832, near Ottawa, at the mouth of Fox river, Illinois; distant 250 miles from place of enrollment. For 60 days.

Name and Rank.	Residence.	Enrolled	Remarks.
Captain.		1832.	
Benj. James	Bond Co	April 17	
First Lieutenant.			
John McAdams	"	"	
Second Lieutenant.			
William Clouse	"	"	
Sergeants.			
A. C. Mackey	"	"	
James Johnston	"	"	
Thomas Price	"	"	
Ephriam M. Gilmore	"	"	
Corporals.			
Elisha Paine	"	"	
David H. Mills	"	"	
Amos Holbrooks	"	"	
Jordan Parker	"	"	
Privates.			
Anthony, Abraham	"	"	
Bradford, James	"	"	
Cruthis, William	"	"	
Dothero, George	"	"	
Durley, James	"	"	Prom. to Q. M. Sergt. of 2d Regt. April 30, '32.
Donee, Thomas C	"	"	
Downing, James	"	"	
Ellison, Elisha	"	"	
Galer, James C	"	"	
Gilmore, John M	"	"	
Gillispie, Josiah R	"	"	
Gill, Francis	"	"	
Glenn, Robert	"	"	
Gilham, Thomas C	"	"	
Gwyne, Hugh B	"	"	Absent on furlough.
Hunter, David	"	"	
Harlin, William	"	"	
Hooper, James D	"	"	
Hooper, Thomas K	"	"	
Jones, Felix	"	"	
Lugg, Noah A	"	"	
Lucas, John	"	"	
Lyles, J. E	"	"	
McAdams, Jas	"	"	
McAdams, Jesse	"	"	
McAdams, Sloss	"	"	
McAdams, William	"	"	
Morgan, Jonathan	"	"	
Mills, A. O. H. P	"	"	
Mullican, James	"	"	
McClure, Eleazer	"	"	
Nicholas, Russell B	"	"	
Pender, Andrew	"	"	
Robinson, Lawson H	"	"	
Royer, Daniel	"	"	
Roberts, Calvert	"	"	Promoted Sergt. Major, April 30, 1832.
Sellers, Benjamin F	"	"	
Volentine, Jackson O	"	"	
West, John	"	"	
Wolard, James B	"	"	Appointed trumpeter, April 30, 1832.
Walker, James	"	"	
Walker, John T	"	"	

Capt. Jeremiah Smith's Company

Of the 2d Regiment, commanded by Col. Jacob Fry, of the Brigade of Mounted Volunteers of Illinois Militia, commanded by Brig.-Gen. Samuel Whitesides. Mustered out of the service of the United States, at the mouth of Fox river, on the 27th day of May, 1832. Place of organization, Whitehall, Greene county, Ill. Distance, 220 miles.

Name and Rank.	Residence.	Enrolled	Remarks.
Captain.		1832.	
Jeremiah Smith	Greene Co.	April 20.	Elected April 20, 1832.
First Lieutenant.			
James Allen	"	"	Elected April 20, 1832.
Second Lieutenant.			
Jacob Wagner	"	"	Elected April 20, 1832.
Sergeants.			
Andrew Guest	"	"	Elected April 20, 1832.
Gregory Doil	"	"	" "
Wm. Thompson	"	"	" "
Peter Thompson	"	"	" "
Corporals.			
Elihu Brown	"	"	Elected April 20, 1832.
Hardy Allen	"	"	" "
George Woods	"	"	" " on furlough.
H. K. Stubblefield	"	"	" "
Privates.			
Broom, Wm	"	"	
Bundy, Horatio	"	"	
Baker, John	"	"	
Buman, Samuel	"	"	Disappeared from the day of enrollment.
Crabtree, Benjamin	"	"	
Campbell, John G	"	"	Sick.
Campbell, John	"	"	
Coats, Richard	"	"	
Carter, Harris	"	"	
Dunsworth, Chas	"	"	
Dollerhite, Jackson	"	"	
Fisher, James	"	"	
Godwin, Jacob	"	"	
Hodges, James	"	"	On furlough.
How, David	"	"	
Hamilton, John	"	"	Sick.
Hawkins, Bevis	"	"	On furlough.
Lorton, Moritica D	"	"	
Lipincut, John	"	"	Deserted.
Miller, John	"	"	
Monday, Samuel	"	"	
Williams, Wm	"	"	
Young, Robert	"	"	

THIRD REGIMENT.

Capt. John Harris' Company,

3d Regiment, commanded by Col. Abram B. Dewitt, of the Brigade of Mounted Volunteers of Illinois Militia, commanded by Brig.-Gen. Samuel Whitesides. Mustered out of the service of the United States, at the mouth of the Fox river, Illinois, May 27, 1832; distant 246 miles from Carlinville, the place of enrollment.

Name and Rank.	Residence.	Enrolled	Remarks.
Captain. John Harris............	Carlinville. Macoupin Co.	1832. April 20.	
First Lieutenant. William G. Coop.....	"	"	
Second Lieutenant. Jeff. Weatherford ...	"	"	
Sergeants.			
Aquilla P. Peppedim	"	"	
John Lewis.........	"	"	
Wilford Palmer.....	"	"	
Travis Moore.......	"	"	
Corporals.			
Geo. W. Cox........	"	"	
Henry H. Havren....	"	"	
Samuel W. McVay...	"	"	
Joshua Martin......	"	"	
Privates.			
Allen, John.........	"	"	
Bayless, John.......	"	"	
Bayless, Rees.......	"	"	
Butler, James.......	"	"	Horse lost—strayed or stolen—value, $35.....
Coop, John.........	"	"	Horse died from forced march; value, $68....
Coop, Ransom.......	"	"	
Driskell, Miles......	"	"	
Davis, Thedorus....	"	"	
English, Irum......	"	"	
English, Levin N....	"	"	Appointed Q. M. Sergeant April 27, 1832.......
Fallum, William.....	"	"	
Foss, Joseph........	"	"	
Hill, Wyatt R.......	"	"	
Hall, Oliver........	"	"	
Hall, James T.......	"	"	Horse gave out on forced march; value, $40..
Harris, Robert......	"	"	
Matthews, Geo......	"	"	
McVay, Healy W ...	"	"	
Miller, Alexander B.	"	"	
Powell, John.......	"	"	
Rhea, Henry D.....	"	"	
Richardson, Larkin.	"	"	
Solomon, Lewis	"	"	
Thurman, Thomas..	"	"	
Weatherford, Hardin	"	"	
Wall, Richard.......	"	"	

CAPTAIN BENJAMIN BARNEY'S COMPANY

Of the 3d Regiment, commanded by Col. Abram B. Dewitt, of the Brigade of Mounted Volunteers commanded by Brig.-Gen. Whitesides. Mustered out of the service, at the mouth of Fox river, on May 27, 1832. Distant 250 miles from the place of enrollment.

Name and Rank.	Residence.	Enrolled	Remarks.
Captains.		1832.	
William Ross......	Atlas, Pike Co.....	April 29.	Captain from April 20th to 28th, 1832.
Benjamin Barney...	"	"	1st Lieut. to the 28th, then elected Captain...
First Lieutenant.			
Israel N. Bert......	"	"	Elected April 28, 1832.
Second Lieutenant.			
Lewis Allen........	"	"	Elected April 28, 1832.
Sergeants.			
Bridge Whitton.....	"	"	Elected April 28, 1832.
Hawins Judd.......	"	"	" "
Eli Hubbard........	"	"	" "
Hansel G. Horn.....	"	"	" "
Corporals.			
Allen B. Lucas.....	"	"	Elected April 28, 1832.
Mathias Bailey.....	"	"	" "
William Mallory....	"	"	" " absent on furlough
Jesse Luster.......	"	"	" " horse strayed or stolen.
Privates.			
Allen, Jonathan B...			
Adney, William.....			Absent on furlough
Blair, William......			
Bush, Alfred.......			
Card, Joseph.......			
Coffee, Meredith W..			
Davis, Robert......			Appointed Sergeant-Major April 29, 1832.
Gall, Joseph.......			
Garrison, Louis A...			
Haze, Robert.......			
Hull, David........			
Haskins, Eliphalet..			
Kannada, Charles...			
Lay, Willis.........			
Lewis, Chidister B..			
Love, Samuel W....			
Lucas, Jesse.......			
McAtee, John.......			
McAtee, Andrew....			Appointed Paymaster April 29, 1832.
Marrow, Richard....			
Meredith, Adair C...			Horse, valued at $60, strayed or stolen
Mize, Samuel P.....			
O'Neil, James......			
Perkins, John......			
Prewitt, St. Clair...			
Swiney, Emory.....			
Shipman, Stephen..			Left sick, on the march
Tolbert, Lindsay....			
Wilson, Austin.....			
Wells, Lucius......			

CAPT. ELISHA PETTY'S COMPANY

Of the 3d Regiment, commanded by Col. Abraham B. Dewitt, of the Brigade of Mounted Volunteers of Illinois Militia, commanded by Brig.-Gen. Samuel Whitesides. Mustered out of the service at the mouth of Fox river May 27, 1832. Distance, 250 miles from place of enrollment.

Name and Rank.	Residence.	Enrolled	Remarks.
Captain.		1832.	
Elisha Petty........	Atlas, Pike Co.....	April 20	Elected April 28, 1832.
First Lieutenant.			
James Ross........	"	"	Elected April 28, 1832.
Second Lieutenant.			
John W. Birch......	"	"	Elected April 28, 1832.

Name and Rank.	Residence.	Enrolled	Remarks.
Sergeants.	Atlas,	1832.	
Joab Brooks	Pike Co	April 20	Elected April 28, 1832.
Gillham Bailey	"	"	"
Joel Harpole	"	"	"
Cornelius Jones	"	"	"
Corporals.			
William Kinman	"	"	Elected April 28, 1832.
William Gates	"	"	"
Ira Shelly	"	"	"
James Woosley	"	"	"
Privates.			
Andrews, Ira	"	"	
Buchalew, Garet	"	"	
Bailey, Caleb	"	"	
Coleman, Franklin P.	"	"	
Cavender, Joseph	"	"	
Decker, Harrison	"	"	
Edwards, Thomas	"	"	Horse, valued at $70, broke down on march.
Fugate, Benj.	"	"	
Greer, James	"	"	
Grimshaw, Edwin	"	"	
Hubbard, Appolis	"	"	
Hume, Berry	"	"	Horse, valued at $65, strayed or stolen.
Jackson, Francis	"	"	
Jeffers, Samuel	"	"	
Kinman, Sims	"	"	
Kinman, Hiram	"	"	
Kinney, Thomas	"	"	
Lynch, William	"	"	
McLintock, Joseph	"	"	Gun, val. $18, bursted; fired by com'nd of Col.
Main, Solomon	"	"	
More, Thomas	"	"	
Mays, Mathew	"	"	
Parkis, Owen	"	"	
Riggs, Samuel	"	"	
Triplet, Nathaniel C.	"	"	
Wadsworth, William	"	"	

CAPT. WILLIAM B. SMITH'S COMPANY

Of the 3d Regiment, commanded by Col. Abraham B. Dewitt, of the Brigade of Mounted Volunteers commanded by Brigadier-General Samuel Whitesides. Mustered out of the service of the United States at the mouth of Fox river, on the Illinois River, on May 27, 1832, being 200 miles distant from place of enrollment.

Name and Rank.	Residence.	Enrolled	Remarks.
Captain.	Morgan Co.	1832.	
William B. Smith	Jacksonville	April 21	
First Lieutenant.			
Starkey R. Powell	"	"	Lost horse on march; appraised at $60.
Second Lieutenant.			
Willie Myers	"	"	
Sergeants.			
Samuel Givens	"	"	
Richard Nelson	"	"	
Peter Barker	"	"	
Wingate I. Numens	"	"	
Corporals.			
Abraham N. Mills	"	"	Gun bursted while firing, by order; value, $20
Thomas Shepherd	"	"	
Felix Ray	"	"	
London C. Ragan	"	"	
Privates.			
Black, William	"	"	Lost his horse on march; appraised at $45.
Bennel, Gabriel E.	"	"	

Name and Rank.	Residence.	Enrolled	Remarks.
		1832.	
Bristow, Thomas....	Jacksonville..	April 21	
Chapman, Isaac.....	"	"	
Connell, Murray Mc	"	"	Appointed Adjutant of 3d Regt. April 27, 1832..
Denton, Robt. H.....	"	"	Farrier of the
Dewitt, Abraham B..	"	"	El'ct'd and app'ted Col. 3d " " "
Flynn, Zadick W.....	"	"	
Holland, Berry......	"	"	
Hardin, John J......	"	"	High private.............................
Hall, Aquilla.......	"	"	
Laughrey, John.....	"	"	
McCall, Arris.......	"	"	
McKee, James.......	"	"	
Miller, William.....	"	"	
Orre, Richard	"	"	Left sick on the march, and furl'd at Dixon's.
Orear, George	"	"	Appointed Quartermaster 3d Regt. April 27, '32
Potts, Joel.........	"	"	
Provines, James.....	"	"	
Plasters, Lemmon...	"	"	Detailed into service of Commander-in-Chief
Roberts, William....	"	"	
Runsdell, Charles...	"	"	
Smith, George.......	"	"	Left sick on march; furl'ed at Dixon's Ferry.
Smith, Laurence	"	"	Detailed by Quartermaster-Gen, as cook.....
Smith, Thomas......	"	"	Furl'd to attend sick at Dixon's Ferry.......
Willson, James......	"	"	

Capt. Nathan Winters' Company

Of the 3d Regiment, commanded by Colonel Abram B. Dewitt, of the Brigade of Mounted Volunteers of Illinois commanded by Brig.-Gen. Samuel Whitesides. Mustered out of the service of the United States, at the mouth of Fox river, on the 27th day of May, 1832. Distance, 215 miles from place of enrollment.

Name and Rank.	Residence.	Enrolled	Remarks.
Captain.	Brown and	1832.	
Nathan Winters.....	Morgan Cos..	April 21.	Elected April 21, 1832 ....
First Lieutenant.			
John D. Pinson......	"	"	Elected April 21, 1832 ....
Second Lieutenant.			
John L. Kirkpatrick.	"	"	Elected April 21, 1832 ....
Sergeants.			
Leander J. Walker..	"	"	Elected April 21, 1832
William D. Johnson.	"	"	" " " "
David Grattan	"	"	" " " "
Thomas J. Cox	"	"	" " " "
Corporals.			
Asa C. Earle	"	"	Elected April 21, 1832
Bird Smith	"	"	" " " "
James F. New	"	"	" " " "
George W. Sawyer..	"	"	" " " "
Privates.			
Asher, William	"	"	
Adams, James	"	"	Horse lost, valued at $40...................
Axby, John	"	"	$70
Beall, Alexander ...	"	"	Elected Major April 29, 1832
Beasley, Benjamin..	"	"	Absent on furlough ....
Black, Jefferson.....	"	"	
Bell, Arthur.........	"	"	
Brown, Cornelius ...	"	"	
Carson, John	"	"	
Cox, William G......	"	"	
Crisp, Benjamin.....	"	"	
Campbell, James G.	"	"	
Cooper, Asa.........	"	"	
Coults, William.....	"	"	
Campbell, David ...	"	"	
Dew, Joseph	"	"	Detailed as a wagoner.....................

Name and Rank.	Residence.	Enrolled	Remarks.
Dixon, Thomas	Brown and Morgan Cos.	1832. April 21.	Detailed as a wagoner.
Forsyth, Johnson	"	"	
Fink, Presley	"	"	
Fulton, John	"	"	
Gillham, Thomas M.	"	"	
Greene, William H.	"	"	
Holmes, Curtis	"	"	
Hobson, John	"	"	
James, Henry	"	"	
Johnson, Samuel	"	"	Detailed into service of Commander-in-Chief
Little, Yancy	"	"	
Moore, David	"	"	
McGee, James	"	"	
Neal, Robert D.	"	"	Detailed as a wagoner.
Powell, Elijah	"	"	
Rue, David W.	"	"	
Riggs, James B.	"	"	
Sawyer, James	"	"	
Wells, Albert	"	"	Horse lost, valued at $70.
Wilcher, Stephen	"	"	

FOURTH REGIMENT.

Capt. M. G. Wilson's Company.

Of the 4th Regiment, commanded by Samuel M. Thompson, of the Brigade of Mounted Volunteers commanded by Brig.-Gen. Samuel Whitesides. Mustered out of the service of the United States, at the mouth of Fox river, May 28, 1832; distant 220 miles from place of enrollment.

Name and Rank.	Residence.	Enrolled	Remarks.
Captain.		1832.	
Moses G. Wilson	Rushville, Ill.	April 23.	Elected Major April 30, 1832
First Lieutenant.			
Alex. Hollingsworth	"	"	Lost horse May 22, 1832; award
Second Lieutenant.			
Harvey Skiles	"	"	
Sergeants.			
John B. Watson	"	"	Appointed Adjt. of 4th Regt. April 30, 1832
G. W. P. Maxwell	"	"	" 1st Sergt. April 30; resign'd May 19
Saml. Hollingsworth	"	"	Elected Captain April 30, 1832
I. G. Randall	"	"	Resigned May 19, 1832
Corporals.			
Ava. Hollingsworth	"	"	Resigned April 30, 1832
James Martin	"	"	Appointed 1st Corporal April 30, 1832
David Frayner	"	"	" 2d Sergeant " "
L. B. Skiles	"	"	" 3d Corporal " "
Privates.			
Abbott, Thomas	"	"	Furloughed (sick) May 19, 1832
Abbott, A.	"	"	" (to attend sick) May 19, 1832
Bogart, Samuel	"	"	Appointed 1st Sergt. May 19, 1832; lost horse.
Burnett, William	"	"	
Butler, George	"	"	
Cox, William	"	"	Appointed 4th Corporal April 30, 1832
Collins, Elijah	"	"	Detailed on extra duty
Dunlap, Adam	"	"	Appointed 1st Surgeon's Mate April 30, 1832
Frakes, James	"	"	
Guinn, William	"	"	
Harrison, G. H	"	"	
Hollingsworth, Abe.	"	"	
Hollingsworth, John	"	"	
Holliday, I. S.	"	"	
Hobart, Chauncey	"	"	Appointed 4th Sergeant April 30, 1832
Hills, Gamaliel	"	"	
Horney, Nowlen	"	"	Lost horse May 22, 1832
Hills, Ishmael	"	"	
Horney, Samuel	"	"	Appointed Quartermaster April 30, 1832
Justus, G. W.	"	"	
Kirkham, Ezra	"	"	Lost horse May 22, 1832
Lockhart, William	"	"	
Lane, Rutherford	"	"	Lost horse May 22, 1832
McFadden, John	"	"	Appointed 3d Sergeant May 19, 1832
Murphy, Robert	"	"	Detailed on extra duty
Morgan, John	"	"	
Moore, Willis	"	"	
Naught, George	"	"	
Riley, Daniel	"	"	Lost horse May 22, 1832
Reno, Jonathan	"	"	Appointed 2d Corporal April 30, 1832
Riley, Caleb	"	"	
Skiles, Benjamin	"	"	
Wilson, Wm. L.	"	"	
Wallace, Moses	"	"	
Wright, Henry	"	"	
Williams, Eli	"	"	
Young, William	"	"	Lost horse May 22, 1832

Capt. Wm. C. Ralls' Company

Of the 4th Regiment of Mounted Volunteers, commanded by Col. Samuel M. Thompson, of the Brigade of Mounted Volunteers commanded by Brig.-Gen. Samuel Whitesides. Mustered out of the service of the United States at the mouth of Fox river May 28, 1832; distant from the place of enrollment, 220 miles.

Name and Rank.	Residence.	Enrolled	Remarks.
Captain.		1832.	
Wm. C. Ralls	Rushville, Ill.	April 23	
First Lieutenant.			
James Blackburn		"	Resigned and returned home May 13, 1832.
Second Lieutenant.			
John Stumet		"	Promoted to 1st Lieutenant May 13.
Sergeants.			
John M. Jones		"	
George W. Penney		"	
James Hunter		"	
James P. Hinney		"	Promoted to 2d Lieutenant May 13.
Corporals.			
Theodore Jourdon		"	
Stephen H. St. Cyr		"	
Jeremiah White		"	
Alfred W. McHatten		"	Appointed Sergeant-Major May 18.
Privates.			
Ballard, Noah B			Sick and furloughed May 26.
Bryant, Rosnel			
Briscoe, John			
Boothe, James			
Coonrod, Jefferson			
Combs, Stephen			
Crawford, John D			
Chapman, Johnston	Rushville, Ill.	April 23	
Dewit, Gabl			
Davis, John			
Edmondson, David			
Earnest, Aaron			Detailed in wagon service.
Glenn, Robert H			
Gay, Lewis			
Hayden, Thomas			
Hambaugh, Stephen			Appointed 4th Sergeant May 13.
Hill, James			
Ives, Joll			
Killion, Michael			Sick and furloughed May 26.
Morris, William			
Moore, Daniel			
McKee, William			
Owen, Luke			
Palmer, Benj			
Rose, Wm. B			
Richardson, Jacob			
Richardson, Auron			
Redick, Thos			
Starr, John H			
Sellars, Thomas			
Seaward, Luster			
Till, Fleming			Sick and furloughed May 10.
Van Winkle, Alex			
Vandeventer, Corn's			Furloughed May 26.
Vanvatter, John			Sick and furloughed May 19.
Wilkerson, Jacob			Appointed 4th Corporal May 18.
Wilson, Benj			

Capt. Abraham Lincoln's Company

Of 4th Regiment of Mounted Volunteers, commanded by Brig.-Gen. Samuel Whitesides. Mustered out of the service of the United States at the mouth of Fox river, May 27, 1832.

Name and Rank.	Residence.	Enrolled	Remarks.
Captain.		1832	
Abraham Lincoln	Sangamon Co	April 21	
First Lieutenants.			
Samuel M. Thomps'n	"	"	Resigned April 30,'32; Col. 4th Regt. Ill. Vol...
Second Lieutenant.			
John Brannan	"	"	
Sergeants.			
John Armstrong	"	"	
Tavner B. Anderson	"	"	
George W. Foster	"	"	Transferred to a foot company April 29,1832.
Obediah Morgan	"	"	
Corporals.			
Thomas Comb	"	"	
John Plasters	"	"	Resigned May 29, and served as private since
William F. Berry	"	"	
Alexander Trent	"	"	
Privates.			
Alexander, Urbin			Absent on extra duty
Armstrong, Pleasant			
Anderson, Isaac			
Armstrong, Hugh			Promoted to 1st Lieut. April 30
Barnette, Clardey			
Crete, Valentine			
Cox, Henry			
Cox, Wm			
Clemment, James	Richland	April 21	
Clary, Royal			
Cummins, William			
Clary, William			
Curman, Merritt M			
Dutten, Samuel			
Dobson, Joseph			
Drake, Nathan	Beardstown	April 29	
Erwin, John	Sangamon Co	April 21	Promoted 3d Sergt. vice G. W. Foster, Apr. 29
Elmore, Cyrus			
Elmore, Travice			
Farmer, Lewis W			
Foster, William			Transferred to a foot company April 29.
Green, William			
Gulliher, Isaac	Dixon's Ferry	May 19	
Houghton, John H	Sangamon Co	April 21	
Hadley, Henry			
Holmler, Joseph			
Hoheimer, Wm			Absent on furlough
Heaverer, Jacob			
Jones, Richard			Promoted from the ranks May 2,color-bearer
Jones, John			Absent without leave
Kirkpatrick, Wm			Promoted from the ranks April 30.
King, Allen			
Lamb, Evan T			
Lane, John Y			
Lane, Richard			
Long, Thomas			
Mathews, Bordry			
Meeker, Usil			
Mounce, John			Absent without leave
Marshall, Wm			
Pierce, Thomas			
Pierce, Calvin			
Pierce, Elijah			
Patter, Royal			
Pantier, David M			Absent on furlough
Pierce, Charles			
Plaster, Michael			Absent without leave
Plunkett, Robert S			
Rankin, David			Transferred to foot company May 19, 1832.
Rutledge, John M			
Rutledge, David			

Name and Rank.	Residence.	Enrolled	Remarks.
Sulivan, Eph			
Sulivan, Charles			
Simmons, James			
Sprouce, Wm. T.			Prom'd f'm ranks May 2; guns'h field and staff.
Tebb, Samuel			
Tibb, Joseph			
Warburton, George			
Yardley, James			

FIFTH REGIMENT.

Capt. M. L. Covell's Company

Of Mounted Volunteers, belonging to the 5th Regiment, commanded by Col. James Johnson, of the Brigade of Mounted Volunteers of Illinois Militia commanded by Brig.-Gen. Samuel Whitesides. Mustered out of the service of the United States at the mouth of Fox river, Illinois, on May 27, 1832; distance 130 miles from place of enrollment.

Name and Rank.	Residence.	Enrolled	Remarks.
Captain.		1832.	
M. L. Covell	Bloomington	April 28	
First Lieutenant.			
Asahel Gridley	"	"	Absent with leave
Second Lieutenant.			
Moses Baldwin	"	"	Absent with leave
Sergeants.			
Baley H. Coffee	"	"	Absent with leave
Isaac Murphy	"	"	" "
David Simmons	"	"	" "
Charles Gates	"	"	" "
Corporals.			
Charles Vezay	"	"	Absent with leave
Henry Miller	"	"	
Reuben Dodson	"	"	
James Durley	"	"	Absent with leave
Privates.			
Brown, Thomas	"	"	
Busick, Henry	"	"	Absent with leave
Copes, William	"	"	" "
Conger, Benjamin	"	"	
Dimmet, William	"	"	
Davenport, Isaiah	"	"	
Davis, Alexander	"	"	Absent with leave
Draper, Joseph	"	"	Killed in battle May 14, 1832
Ellis, Martin C.	"	"	Absent with leave
Funk, John	"	"	" "
Gilpin, Samuel	"	"	
Gates, Stephen F.	"	"	
Hurbert, Mathew	"	"	
Hurbert, Robert A.	"	"	Absent with leave
Harris, Robert F.	"	"	" "
Hatten, John	"	"	" "
Isham, John	"	"	" "
Johnson, Charles	"	"	" "
Kimber, Baley	"	"	" "
Landy, John	"	"	
McCullough, William			
McKee, William	"	"	Absent with leave
Oatman, Clement	"	"	
Orrendorff, James	"	"	Absent with leave
Provo, Francis	"	"	
Phillips, James	"	"	
Paul, James	"	"	Absent with leave
Rutledge, Thomas	"	"	
Simpson, Timothy	"	"	" "
Toliver, John	"	"	" "
Vittito, John	"	"	" "
Vandoler, Jesse	"	"	" "
Windham, Reuben	"	"	
Wiley, George	"	"	" "
Young, Anderson	"	"	
Young, Briant	"	"	